Theology Devotional

"*Theology Devotional* is a unique book in the world of devotional works. It is a most welcomed addition. K. Bernard Knutson believes the devotional life and the theological life should be wedded. So do I! This book unites these worlds in a way that will both bless the mind and stir the heart. I enthusiastically commend its widest reading."

—Daniel L. Akin, President, Southeastern Baptist Theological Seminary

"What a wonderful gift K. Bernard Knutson has prepared for followers of Christ! This thoughtfully designed devotional book guides readers toward biblically faithful, theological reflections for each day throughout the year. Beginning or ending each day by meditating on the nature of Scripture, the Trinity, Jesus Christ, the Holy Spirit, salvation, and other key doctrines will strengthen the faith of men and women with God-honoring, doxological thoughts and encouragement for faithful Christian living. It is a joy to recommend this helpful work."

—David S. Dockery, President, Southwestern Baptist Theological Seminary

"This book provides a short daily devotional for each day of the year, focusing on theological terms and doctrines, and the corresponding biblical texts. Each entry includes reflection questions, encouraging the reader to mediate on the subject for the day. In a year's time, the reader will have worked through the major doctrines of the Christian faith. In short, concise, clear, thoughtful daily readings, God's incredible wisdom and grace is revealed and explained. Working through the readings is an act of worship and thus is a valuable daily practice, an opportunity to be shaped and formed by the truth of Scripture and Christian doctrine."

—Glenn R. Kreider, Editor in Chief, *Bibliotheca Sacra*

"K. Bernard Knutson's *Theology Devotional* is a welcome addition to the intersection of theology and spiritual formation. In this thoughtful volume, Knutson guides readers through the foundational categories of Christian doctrine, combining concise theological description with Scripture-driven reflection. Each section invites contemplative engagement—leading the reader from understanding to prayer. As the evangelical world grows increasingly attentive to dogmatic and systematic theology, this devotional shines as a gem—one that nourishes the soul, grounds contemplation in the word, and deepens devotion through a theological lens."

—Joshua R. Farris, Director of Spiritually Driven Leadership, Soul Science Ministries/Institute (with Kairos University)

Theology Devotional

A Daily Study in Systematic Theology

K. BERNARD KNUTSON

RESOURCE *Publications* • Eugene, Oregon

THEOLOGY DEVOTIONAL
A Daily Study in Systematic Theology

Resource Publications
An Imprint of Wipf and Stock Publishers
199 W. 8th Ave., Suite 3
Eugene, OR 97401

www.wipfandstock.com

PAPERBACK ISBN: 979-8-3852-7586-1
HARDCOVER ISBN: 979-8-3852-7587-8
EBOOK ISBN: 979-8-3852-7588-5

To my loving wife,
Sarah

Contents

Preface

This project was conceived out of necessity. When I taught Bible and theology courses at church and school settings, I had to think of ways where Christian laymen, young and old, could come and understand the essential concepts of Christianity without having to go to Bible school and seminary. It is not that I feel that these institutions should not exist. I would not be able to speak about these topics without higher education. My issue was that, where pastors often have the great intention of going to seminary in order to bring the basics of the Bible to their congregation, theological topics are rarely brought down to the everyman from the ivory tower.

Everyone is a theologian, meaning, everyone has a view of God. But every Christian ought to be a good theologian, because we have the right communication from the true God. It makes no sense for us to resort to bad theology because we do not want to "put God in a box." He will never be in one, no matter how much one tries to understand him. Therefore, we might as well try to understand him as much as possible while realizing we will never reach the end of understanding him. Therefore, the question remains: If a Christian *will* think of God, *needs* to think of God, and *ought* to think of God, how can a Christian do so accurately without spending years of their time and treasure in study away at an institution, putting their ministry life on hold?

My hope is that this book is the resource for others that I wish I had when I was new in my faith. I believe this book is a great start for someone in their journey to understand God better as they go through the theological process, and for the pastor or ministry leader who wants to have an easy, yet biblically solid, evangelical resource to use for classes instead of using or recommending a gigantic tome. I was trained that theology must be Biblical in the Protestant tradition, and, that, afterwards, we then must consider the logical, historical, and experiential realities of a theological topic. What I set out to do was to take the average Christian, have them dedicate a month to a particular theological study, and, every day, provide them a working definition of a theological topic, give some relevant Bible verses, state some issues in that topic, and ask a thoughtful question for self-reflection or reflection in a group. I pray that you, the reader, will not be merely informed, but challenged to grow. May God bless you for taking this journey.

In Christ and Christ in,
K. Bernard Knutson

Acknowledgments

First, I thank God.

Second, I thank the publisher, Resource Publications and Wipf & Stock for giving me this opportunity. Thanks to Matthew Wimer, George Callihan, Joe Delahanty, Elisabeth Rickard, Karlie Tedrick, Heather Carraher, and the rest of the team.

Third, I would like to thank the pastors and leaders that have encouraged me and who have given me opportunities through the years. Brent and Sarah for noticing the calling on my life. Nick and Dawn for encouragement in hard times. Jose and Elaine for providing flexibility and opportunity. Thank you Sean and Maria for your friendship and support.

Fourth, I would like to thank all of the theology, philosophy, and history professors that put up with me asking questions (and to go back a slide in their presentation): Adam Demark, Dave Hodgdon, Scott Knievel, Ron Lindsey, Ernie Richards, Jody Riethmiller, Jason Weaver, Mike Winters, David B. Finkbeiner, Bryan M. Litfin, Michael McDuffee, Winfred Neely, Bryan O'Neal, Gregg Quiggle, Tim Sigler, and Todd Saur. You will all have amazing rewards to place at Jesus' feet when you go home. I am indebted to you all.

Finally, I want to thank my family. Although I am humbled to be the heir my Grandparents Jack and Margo Knutson, as well as Grandpa Howard Morarie, I want to thank my Grandma Maxine Evon Morarie most of all. You have been the greatest example of a life well-lived that I have ever been witness to. Your humble service to the Ayore people has been an incredible example of servant leadership. I thank you for being the premier example of a woman of God. I was able to find an amazing wife from that example. Thanks to you and Grandma Margo for reading to me as a boy all of the fairy tales and missionary stories. You both forced me to make a decision about the Bible stories you read to me, as well, having to place the whole of Scripture into reality or fantasy. And I am thankful to my parents, John and Nancy, for giving me the space to come to the right conclusion on that question. Last but not least, I thank my wife, Sarah. God placed you in my life to be the perfect compliment. You have been the support I have needed every step of the way. Thank you for all you have done for me and our family.

Abbreviations

Genesis	Gen
Exodus	Exod
Leviticus	Lev
Numbers	Num
Deuteronomy	Deut
Joshua	Josh
Judges	Judg
Ruth	Rut
1 Samuel	1 Sam
2 Samuel	2 Sam
1 Kings	1 Kgs
2 Kings	2 Kgs
1 Chronicles	1 Chr
2 Chronicles	2 Chr
Ezra	Ezra
Nehemiah	Neh
Esther	Esth
Job	Job
Psalms	Ps (*pl.* Pss)
Proverbs	Prov
Ecclesiastes	Eccl
Song of Songs	Song
Isaiah	Isa
Jeremiah	Jer
Lamentations	Lam
Ezekial	Ezek
Daniel	Dan
Hosea	Hos

Joel	Joel
Amos	Amos
Obadiah	Obad
Jonah	Jonah
Micah	Mic
Nahum	Nah
Habakkuk	Hab
Zephaniah	Zeph
Haggai	Hag
Zechariah	Zech
Malachi	Mal
Matthew	Matt
Mark	Mark
Luke	Luke
John	John
Acts	Acts
Romans	Rom
1 Corinthians	1 Cor
2 Corinthians	2 Cor
Galatians	Gal
Ephesians	Eph
Philippians	Phil
Colossians	Col
1Thessalonians	1 Thess
2Thessalonians	2 Thess
1 Timothy	1 Tim
2 Timothy	2 Tim
Titus	Titus
Philemon	Phlm
Hebrews	Heb
James	Jas
1 Peter	1 Pet
2 Peter	2 Pet
1 John	1 John
2 John	2 John
3 John	3 John
Jude	Jude
Revelation	Rev

January: The Bible

January 1: Bibliology

Have you ever considered how we got the Bible? Or have you thought about how exactly the Bible is God's Word? What is the Bible? All of these questions can be answered by engaging in bibliology. *Bibliology is the study of the Bible, its properties, and how it came to be.* This discipline is important for the Christian to understand because the Bible is the textual foundation of the Christian faith. Some important issues within bibliology are: who the author(s) of Scripture are, what the Bible is, when was the Bible written and/or compiled, whether we have the text of the Bible today, what are the right books of the Bible, how the we can know the Bible is what it claims to be, and if the Bible is authoritative in what it claims, to name a few. How would you answer these questions?

January 2: Doctrine

A Doctrine is a belief, correct or not, that is held by an individual or a group. Every person has doctrines that they hold onto that are informed by their worldviews. Large groups, like religions and governments, have explicit and implied doctrines that they operate from. People can also act inconsistently with the doctrines they hold. Being aware of the doctrines you hold onto is important because you can then be aware of the motivations of your actions. You can also evaluate what groups align or do not align with your views. But how do you develop doctrines? For the Christian, these are typically based on Scripture, tradition, reason, and experience, which is the Wesleyan Quadrilateral. What doctrines do you hold to? How do you develop your doctrines?

January 3: Methodology

There are many fields of study, and there are many methods one can use for studying different topics, as well. The same can be said of the study of theology. *Methodology is the process in which an operation or study is performed.* If one desires to understand something rightly, one ought to have methodologies that can help them arrive at the most accurate conclusions. Problematic methodologies have been used throughout history to bring about questionable doctrines. A recurring method is to take the supernatural elements out of the Scriptures, which obviously contain supernatural elements. One can plot narrative, analyzes logic, and look at form in poetry, for some examples. A basic method is the inductive Bible study, which looks to observe, interpret, and apply. What method do you use for studying the Bible?

January 4: General Revelation

If God is real, then we should be able to see His handiwork in His creation. *General Revelation is the term for nature telling us about God.* In Romans 1, Paul tells the church that the creation reveals God's "eternal power and Godhead" (Ro. 1:20). Because of this, even though mankind is born sinful and destined for eternal separation from God, and because we know of God and His power, we are also guilty for not seeking Him out. There is a debate that questions, "if we can be damned for our general knowledge of God, can we be saved through it, too?" But the Bible is clear that the Gospel is necessary for salvation (see *Soteriology*). But if God's creation cannot tell us the gospel, where can we turn to get that information about Him? How have you seen God and His power in creation? *Ref.: Ro. 1; Ps. 19*

January 5: Special Revelation

Special Revelation is the term for God telling us about God. God has spoken to mankind in many ways, but the special revelation that He gave to us is the Bible. One question that one may have today is which religion's scripture is right about its god? But, if we consider the accuracy of the Bible compared to any other religious document, we see that it is more reliable historically, geographically, morally, and logically than other religious texts (see *Inerrancy*). And if the Bible is correct about what it says regarding this world, we can trust what it says about the unseen world. Because God gave us one collection of texts to speak about Himself and His desires, we should hold that text in high regard. Do you consider the Scriptures as God's very word to us?

January 6: Hermeneutics

Everyone who tries to understand a piece of art engages in hermeneutics. *Hermeneutics is the study and discipline of interpretation.* Even a painting with red covering the canvas has something it is trying to say. There have historically been two main camps for interpreting the Bible: the allegorical and the literal approach. The allegorical approach puts the audience in charge of finding a hidden meaning behind the text. The literal approach looks to the author's intent to explain a clear meaning the audience must understand plainly. For the Christian, because we are reading God's word, we should seek to find God's meaning if we are to understand His Word. Therefore, the more responsible position is the literal approach. Which method do you use? How can you find the author's intention better in your reading?

January 7: Narrative

A Narrative is a story. Whether a story is true or not, we still tell narratives the same way. Every story has a setting before the story (exposition), the main characters entrance into a particular story (inciting incident), an increase of tension (rising action), the height of tension (climax), the release of tension (falling action), and a new setting after the story's events (resolution). Narratives can have conflict of man vs. man, man vs. self, and man vs. force. Some stories, like Star Wars can have all three. Every story has a *Protagonist, the individual going through the tension*, an *Antagonist, the individual trying to stop the protagonist*, and usually other characters. The Bible is filled with narratives. What are some narrative examples that you can think of?

January 8: Law

A Law is a statute that permits or does not permit something conditionally or unconditionally from cases or command. Laws are important because we all want to live in a fair society. But laws are not just in our physical world. For those familiar with math and science, there are laws that humanity has discovered that have pre-existed mankind. Even morality, what is right and wrong, seems to predate man and is often the basis for civil laws. In the Bible, we call the first five books, Genesis, Exodus, Leviticus, Numbers, and Deuteronomy, the "Law" because God gave Moses and the Israelites laws after they escaped slavery. When we make laws today, they are either based in God's character or not. They are also either based in case study, or they are from authority. How would you determine if a law was just or unjust?

January 9: History

Because the events of the Bible took place in many different periods, we want to understand how those events connect throughout time. The authors of Scripture also knew this, and they documented their own important historical events. *History is the study of events in time.* When we study history, we look at written documents, like the Bible, and the material data we find in archaeology (see *Archaeology*) to have a better account of the past. When the data that we find in both of these areas disagree with each other, we have to see if something is wrong with our understanding of the text or the archaeology. The Bible, though, has a strong degree of agreement between these two areas. Where have you seen the Bible and archaeology agree?

January 10: Poetry

The largest book of the Bible, the Psalms, is a poetry book. Along with the books of Proverbs, Ecclesiastes, Song of Solomon, and Lamentations, poetry makes up about a third of the Old Testament, showing us how important it is for us to understand and appreciate it as a medium for God's Word. *Poetry is artfully arranged literature that typically fits a certain form and meter.* In our modern context, we appreciate rhyme and syllables. Whereas modern, western poetry has been dominated by rhyming forms, Hebrew poetry relies more on *Parallelism*, where *the author will use two words, phrases, or figures of speech to talk about the same issue*. Poetry can be challenging to understand, but its creativity is what makes it an interesting genre to explore. What are some poems that have evoked an emotional response from you?

January 11: Prophecy

If a prophet is one that provides divine communication to man, every human author of Scripture is a prophet in a way. But in the Bible, there is an entire third of the Old Testament that is of the genre called prophecy. *Prophecy is divine communication that often foretells or forthtells of a blessing or a judgment.* There are few ways the prophetic books can be divided. First, there are the major prophets (Isaiah, Jeremiah, Lamentations, Ezekiel, and Daniel) and the minor prophets (Hosea-Malachi). Another way to look at the prophets is to see the prophets before, during, and after the exile. Some prophets *Foretell*, or *speak about the future*, and some *Forthtell*, or *speak about events that have happened in the past or present*. Some Old Testament prophecies even speak of Jesus. What are some of your favorite prophecies in the Bible?

January 12: Apocalypse

Apocalypse means "unveiling," much like the game shows that pull back a curtain on a mystery gift. We translate a famous book of the Bible called "Apocalypse" similarly: Revelation. For texts inside and outside the Bible, *Apocalypses are texts that tell stories about the end times and supernatural realms often with vivid imagery using types.* A famous extra-biblical example of a book that contains the apocalyptic genre would be the book of Enoch, and an Old Testament example is the book of Daniel. These books use types to speak about the future. Theologians use this literature to form views on eschatology (see *Eschatology*). Apocalyptic literature is often used to motivate its original audience to be mindful of judgments as well as see hope in the future. For example, when you read Revelation 21, do you feel joy or sorrow?

January 13: Gospels

A Gospel is a genre of literature that tells of the life and ministry of Jesus. The Gospels are historical texts and are the only authoritative, inspired sources of Jesus' life and ministry here on earth. Four Gospels speak of Jesus in slightly different ways and to different audiences. Matthew speaks of Jesus as the King of the Jews to a Jewish audience, Mark speaks of Jesus as a suffering servant to Rome, Luke speaks of Jesus as the Son of Man to a gentile audience, and John speaks of Jesus as the Son of God to all non-believers. False Gospels, like the Gospel of Thomas and the Gospel of Peter, support the true Gospel accounts by confirming that they do not speak in depth on subjects like Jesus' childhood and His coming out of the tomb. What is your favorite Gospel?

January 14: Parables

A Parable is an extended metaphor, mostly in a narrative, that often leads to a moral teaching. Jesus makes a lot of use of parables in His teachings. He uses at least thirty parables to teach about Himself, His relationships with His followers, and even about events in the end times. Jesus used simple things like seeds (Matt. 13:1–8, 31–32; Mark 4:26–29), plants (Matt. 13:24–30; Luke 13:6–9), coins (Matt. 13:44; 25:13–30; Matt. 21:33–46; Luke 15:8–10; 19:11–27;), social status (Luke 10:30–37; 17:7–10), and relationships (Luke 15:11–32) as illustrations. There are even parables in the Old Testament, with one example given by Nathan to David about David's cruelty (2 Sa. 12:1–7). Parables can be difficult to decipher without knowing what all the metaphors are, so they often take thought to consider. What are some of your favorite parables in the Bible?

January 15: Epistles

Epistles are the primary teaching tool of the apostles during their ministry. *An Epistle is a letter.* We have epistles from John, Paul, Jude, James, and Peter. The epistle to the Hebrews is anonymous, and, even though we do not know the author, it is canonical and contains much of the same theology that Paul taught. Because epistles are correspondence between two people or a person to a group, it is important that we are not only familiar with the author, but also with the audience being written to. The authors make a lot of use of logic in their writings, and the letters often have praise and admonitions for their audience. Although Christians today were not the original audience, we can still receive the same timeless principles as our brethren in the past. What is an epistle that encourages or motivates you?

January 16: Logic

All communication is based on logical reasoning. In fact, we use logic every day in our conversations without even trying. *Logic is the use of right thinking in deductive and inductive arguments.* The laws of logic are: 1) Identity (A is A), 2) Non-Contradiction (A is not Non-A), and 3) Excluded Middle (Either A or Non-A). *Deductive arguments use premises to arrive at conclusions. Inductive arguments are arguments built on case and probability.* Deduction can have premises follow (valid) or not (invalid), and those premises can be true (sound) or not (unsound). Induction can have probable arguments (strong) or not (weak), and have true arguments (cogent) or not (uncogent). Where do you see the authors of Scripture using logic?

January 17: Manuscript Tradition

A Manuscript Tradition is a collection of manuscripts with a lineage of similar transmission. For the New Testament, there are different text families: the Byzantine (which has the most copies), the Western, and the Alexandrian (which has the oldest copies). Furthermore, there is the Textus Receptus, a sixteenth century compilation using Byzantine manuscripts, and the eclectic text, which is a modern compilation of the Alexandrian manuscripts. Every classical book has some sort of manuscript tradition, but none with the pedigree of the New Testament. There are more than 5,000 Greek manuscripts for the NT, and some are less than a hundred years from the original writing. To compare, the Iliad has 643 manuscripts with the oldest being 500 years after it was supposed to be written. Does this fact bring you comfort when you read your Bible?

January 18: Textual Criticism

Because the King James Bible uses the Textus Receptus and every other modern translation uses the eclectic text, there are some differences between the KJV and the other modern translations, none of which change Christian doctrine. We know these differences because of textual criticism. *Textual Criticism is the process of finding the history and legitimacy of a textual document.* The oldest manuscripts were written with uppercase letters, or majuscules and uncials (from the second to the eighth century). Then came minuscule, or lowercase letters (from the eighth to the sixteenth century). This helps us know how far back a reading goes. Scholars tend to prize older texts with difficult readings. Look in your Bibles to see what text families are used.

January 19: Canonicity

The term canon comes from a reed used as a standard of measurement in the ancient Near East. Therefore, *the Canonicity of something is the understanding of whether a piece of media fits the standard of a specific group.* Because the Bible is a collection of books, the question becomes how those particular books are determined as canon. But the canon of Scripture is not something chosen arbitrarily or out of preference. Because the Old and New Testament books were written by prophets and apostles respectively, it is those books that are discovered and recognized as authoritative that Christians acknowledge as canon. This is more like archaeology than construction. The Bible is also self-referential, as the NT authors often cite the canon of the OT. What OT quote in the NT is your favorite? *Ref.: Heb. 1:1–3; Matt.12:40*

January 20: Human Authorship

The *Confluence of Scripture is the doctrine that states the Bible has a human and divine authorship. Human Authorship is the understanding that the Bible is in part a product of human abilities.* From the human contribution, God uses the various human authors' languages, artistic styles, and vantage points from their historical contexts to bring about the inspired Scriptures. This means the Bible is a product of people from different centuries, three continents (Asia, Africa, and Europe), three languages (Hebrew, Aramaic, and Greek), both rich and poor, and from people of various occupations. There are voices of men and women who lament and rejoice, and texts of poetry, prophecy, history, and law, to name a few genres. It is fascinating that all these authors agree. What do you appreciate about the human aspect of Scripture?

January 21: Divine Authorship

In the confluence of Scripture, *Divine Authorship is the understanding that the Bible is a product of Godly communication.* We can call the Bible "the Word of God" because it is literally His communication to us. The Bible is not just any book. It is a holy, authoritative text that communicates everything that humans need to know about God and how we are to be in right relationship with Him. In the Old Testament, there are many prophets that reveal God as their source in their statement, "Thus says the Lord…." In the New Testament, we have the words of Jesus, the Son, as well as inspired apostolic writings. This collected written testimony of God is the reason we can put our trust in Scripture and not another source. How has God's Word made a positive impact in your life?

January 22: Inspiration

Inspiration is the doctrine that articulates the Bible's original document as being God's very Word. This doctrine comes from the translation of *theopneustos*, or God-breathed, in 2 Timothy 3:16. It is important to understand that the only inspired text is the original autograph of the Scriptures that was written by an inspired author. Every other copy of that text, whether in the original language or as a translation, is not inspired. But as Christians, we can be thankful to have such a faithful transmission of the Old and New Testament texts, as well as a large collection of scholarly translations, so that we can be sure that what we have today captures the same words and meaning respectively that the inspired authors originally wrote down. How can the doctrine of inspiration provide believers with assurance that God's Word is authoritative?

January 23: Inerrancy

Inerrancy is the doctrine that articulates that the Bible's original document is without error. The logic of inerrancy is this: the Bible is God's Word, God cannot err, therefore, God's Word cannot err. It is often suggested that this is argument is circular, as God not being able to err is found within God's Word. But we can also arrive at this conclusion through the ontological argument, which states if God is all good and all powerful, it is necessary that He exists, because it is not good or powerful to not exist. And if God is good, He cannot err. The supposed contradictions of the text often come down to parallel accounts, unknown historical details, and issues with ancient science. Do these issues deal with the reader or God's account? *Ref. Titus 1:2*

January 24: Infallibility

The general goal of Scripture is to tell us our need of and the means of salvation. But can the Bible fail in this endeavor? *Infallibility is the doctrine that articulates the Bible's original document cannot fail in what it sets out to do or lead one astray.* Therefore, the doctrine of infallibility teaches that if the Bible is truly God's Word, it cannot fail, and has not failed in its mission. The Bible can also not be made impotent (indefeasibility) or destroyed forever (indestructibility). Because we get a glimpse into the future of the world in the Bible, we know that God is ultimately victorious over sin and death, and that every tribe, tongue, and nation will stand before Him (Rev. 7:9). How does God's Word bring you comfort knowing God will be successful in our lives? *Ref. Isa. 55:11; John 10:35*

January 25: Inexhaustibility

Inexhaustibility, also called indefatigability, *is the doctrine that articulates that the Bible cannot be studied in finality.* There are many fascinating texts throughout history that compel scholars to research and write many books and articles to further understand them. It is exciting to uncover a lost book or tablet and discover new things. But ultimately, these texts hit a limit of interest and are studied into the ground. The Bible is not like this. John tells us, just of Jesus' life alone, that countless books could be written about it (John 21:25). Also, great works of art, like the works of Shakespeare, can inspire us to do great things, but they cannot positively change a person's life, or bring them to right relationship with God like Scripture can. What in Scripture has rewarded you through multiple readings? *Ref. John 21:25; 1 Pe. 1:23*

January 26: Authority

There are many authorities of truth. In modernity, math and science tend to be the authorities we trust the most. Those work well for understanding the physical world, but how do we understand non-physical reality? *The Authority of Scripture is the doctrine that teaches the Bible is an authority on what it speaks on.* Because God is immaterial, we cannot use physical tools to know Him. Therefore, we need communication from Him to understand who He is and what He wants. Authorities like math and science, can show us that there is a Creator, but not who He is. Some want to know God, but not through the Bible. But if you took the Bible away, what other source would exist to teach us the things we need to know about Him?

January 27: Sufficiency

The Sufficiency of Scripture is the teaching that the Bible tells us everything that we need to know about God and what He wants from us. The Bible does not tell us everything we want to know. We may want to know exactly how many angels there are, or what exactly was said on the road to Emmaus. But the Bible only tells us what we need to know. Not only that, but it tells us everything that we absolutely need to know in this life about God. Theology, as part of its task, is to make sense of the parts of Scripture that are implied or to make logical connections to better understand the things of God. We can hold to logical conclusions, but ultimately, theology is based on the clear truths of Scripture because that is the ultimate source we have. It is also the standard God holds us to. How has God's Word been sufficient in your reading?

January 28: Perspicuity

The Perspicuity, or clarity, *of Scripture is the doctrine that tells us the Bible is able to be clearly understood.* One may not understand a book due to reading comprehension. In this way, the Bible is the same as the works of Jane Austin or a math book. But God intended the Bible to be understood by people. There are no mysterious or cryptic messages that we have to decipher within the pages of the Bible to be a Christian. This does not mean that there are no difficult passages, but the Bible was given to man by God to be read and understood for what it is clearly saying. This is so everyone can understand God's desires. If there are difficulties, one could always try an easier translation or audio book. What is a passage that is or used to be difficult for you?

January 29: Translation

Translation is the art and science of taking words in one language and communicating them in a different language. Words have a range of meaning. In English, "trunk" can be a nose, a dead tree, and a suitcase. Because no two languages have words that perfectly translate from one to another, whenever a person or committee translates a text, there are many decisions that have to be made. Because the Bible has many words with important meaning, the problems are greater. When translating the Bible, we have three broad categories: word-for-word translations (formal equivalence), thought-for-thought translations (dynamic equivalence), and paraphrases. All have their purposes, but the most important thing is the meaning of the God's Word. Often the best solution is to read many translations. What is your favorite translation?

January 30: Jesus the Word

Where the Bible is the special revelation of God, *Jesus the Word is the ultimate revelation of God.* Jesus' being the Word, or *logos*, of God is a doctrine that is taught in the Gospel of John. This idea seems to indicate that not only is Jesus is a form of God's revelation, as Jesus' taking on humanity shows us that He is God, but He is also part of the Trinity, and, therefore, was present during creation in His divine nature. John's inclusion of this doctrine at the beginning of his gospel instead of speaking about Jesus' nativity shows that he does not want the reader to think about Jesus' taking a human nature, but to know that Jesus has always had a divine nature and is Creator. Jesus said when we see Him, we see the Father, as we see can actually see the divine looking at Jesus. *Ref. John 1:1–5; 14:9*

January 31: Creeds

What were Christians taught before the New Testament was written? The obvious answer is the Old Testament and various teachings of Jesus that were passed on by the apostles. But the early church also recited creeds. *Creeds are formal statements of belief that are held by various groups of Christians.* Although the oldest complete creed we have today is the Apostle's Creed, there are examples of a creed or creeds that predate the completion of the New Testament. These creeds tend to be runs of doctrinal teachings regarding Christ's death, burial, and resurrection, as well as other beliefs about God and the end times. Many evangelical churches today are non-creedal, but there are protestant denominations that still recite creeds. What creeds does your church hold to? *Ref. 1 Cor. 15:3–4; Phil. 2:6–11; 1 Tim. 2:5; 3:16; 1 Pet. 3:18; 1 John 2:22, 5:1*

February: Humanity

February 1: Anthropology

Anthropology is the study of humanity. *Theological Anthropology is the discipline of seeing humanity not as just biological creatures but more from a scriptural point of view.* Both nature and Scripture suggest that man is more than the sum of the cells that make up his physical body. If ethics, for example, were just a matter of cultural convenience, there would be no objective good or bad, defeating the reason for the category. Therefore, what drives a person to live by and be connected to an ethical standard beyond their cells, brainwaves, and social groups? The Bible, unlike nature or the philosophies of man, suggests a reason for this drive and connection. What are some ways the Bible tells us we are more than just our physical bodies?

February 2: Archaeology

Archaeology makes up one half of the study of history. Therefore, if we want to understand the Bible and its history, we need to aware of archaeology. *Archaeology is the study of the material data of ancient civilizations.* For some archaeologists, there is more of an interest in ancient languages, or philology. The civilizations of the *Ancient Near East*, or *the Middle East before the rise of Christianity and Islam*, are the societies Christians are interested in studying. This includes understanding the Israelite and Canaanite groups of ancient Israel, but also includes Egypt and the city states of the Fertile Crescent. Look into the Merneptah Stele, the Meshe Stele, Sennacherib's Prism, and Cyrus' Cylinder for examples. How can archaeology help deepen your faith?

February 3: Life

Life, at its most basic scientific definition, *is the experience of animate creatures.* But the experience of plant life is demonstrably different than that of an ant, or a bird, or a human being. In Scripture, life is often contrasted with death. In the same way that there are gradations of lived experience among animate life, because there are many kinds of death (See *Death*), life has gradation for us as human beings. We have the common experience humanity has on earth. We can also gain a new life when we become Christians. This new life is not a biological metamorphosis, but a Spiritual transformation that is not necessarily experiential but nonetheless real. Finally, there is eternal life in heaven that we can have if we partake of the new life in Christ. How is your life different than other living creatures? *Ref. 2 Cor. 5:17; John 3:16*

February 4: Creature

A Creature is any living thing created by God. In biology, we can know there are many kinds of creatures on earth that we can study using observation. But what we can understand about living creatures using observation has its limits. There are also creatures referenced in Scripture that are not biological, but spiritual. Therefore, the Scriptures are another source in understanding created beings. Many cultures may be aware of these supernatural creatures, but they can only be truly understood through the special revelation of Scripture. Also, we cannot understand the spiritual nature of animals through natural means, but Scripture speaks of some animals as, or having, a soul. What can you learn about creatures from Scripture? *Ref. Ps. 148; Eccl. 3:21*

February 5: Person

In philosophy, *a Person is a being with or having the capacity for their own mind, will, and emotions.* A person is different from other animate creatures in that they or their species has realized autonomy. Human beings are personal, but they are not the only persons documented in Scripture. Angelic beings are persons as they are often described as having mind, will, and emotions in the Bible. The triune God of the Bible is also personal. In fact, there are three persons that make up the Triune God: the Father, the Son, and the Holy Spirit. In both the Old Testament and New Testament, the members of the Godhead can be seen as distinct persons with separate minds, wills, and emotions, yet they are all described as God. How can someone determine who has personhood and who does not? *Ref. Mark 12:30; Eph. 4:30; 2 Tim. 2:26*

February 6: Humanity

There are some questions that nature cannot answer for us. When and how did matter come from non-matter, life come from non-life, and humanity come from non-humanity? The last of these is paramount in theological anthropology. *Humans are persons with a physical and spiritual makeup, made in God's image, with the capacity for gaining righteousness in Christ.* In Scripture, mankind was created as unique by God, responsible for caring for creation. Since the Fall, mankind has been at odds with God and in need of spiritual intervention to have relationship restored. In the first century AD, the eternal Son of God took on a human nature in order to live a perfect life, die, resurrect, and be glorified to repair that relationship. How do the traits of mankind make humanity unique? *Ref. Gen 1–3; Gospels*

February 7: Imago Dei

The Imago Dei *is the doctrine that explains how mankind is unique in creation in having Godly attributes.* The Bible tells us in Genesis that man was created in the "image of God." This does not mean that we are physical replicas of God. Instead, where God has unlimited attributes, humans have attributes in a finite way. For example, God is omnipresent, but we are physically located in one place. With ANE idol-making reversed, God made man in His image instead of humanity making an image of God. The image of God has been articulated in many ways, but the commonalities are that humans are distinct, equal, have dignity, able to have unique relationship with God, and that Christ is the ultimate image of God. How does someone bear God's image in your understanding? *Ref. Gen. 1:26, 27; 9:6*

February 8: Adam and Eve

Adam and Eve are the first people that God created according to Scripture. Everyone that descends from Adam and Eve will carry on their characteristics. There are some Christians who, appealing to scientific conclusions over Scripture, have attempted to find a "historical Adam" in a hominin or in a special selection of hominins other than homo sapiens. But what is Genesis 1–11 saying if things happened differently than what these chapters say? The ideas in these chapters, God creating everything, humanity being made in God's image, the origin of sin, the reality of the Flood, are all brought into question when the literal reading is cast aside. How can we be open to scientific conclusions about the origins of humanity while maintaining the integrity of Scripture?

February 9: Monism

Monism is the view that the cosmos has only one aspect – physical or spiritual. Apart from the Judeo-Christian religions, monism is the dominant view in both the global East and West. In Europe and North America, physical monism is a popular belief, as it is the view of atheists and agnostics. Because the sciences can only analyze the physical world, it would follow that some who hold science over philosophy would believe we are only physical. One issue here is that claims like "the scientific method is superior in finding truth" cannot be proven using the scientific method. In the East, however, spiritual monism is the most common view. Here, religions like Hinduism and Buddhism believe the physical is merely an illusion, and that the cosmos is actually spiritual. Why are these views contrary to the Bible?

February 10: Dualism

Dualism is the view that the cosmos has two aspects – physical and spiritual. The Abrahamic religions are all dualistic because they acknowledge both a spiritual and physical component to reality. Not only do they believe that people have a spiritual and physical nature, but they also believe that strictly spiritual creatures exist. These worldviews also believe that there are physical and spiritual realms. The universe is physical, but we also know of the spiritual realms of heaven and hell from special revelation (see *Special Revelation*). A problem with monism compared to dualism is that there is often no distinction amongst things in the world. A dog, a baby, a star, and an atom are all of equal importance or irrelevance. How does the Bible support dualism?

February 11: Spirit

The Hebrew word *ruach* and the Greek term *pneuma* are both terms that translate to wind, breath, and spirit. *The Spirit is the metaphysical component of a person.* The spiritual part of man is made up of a bunch of different metaphysical aspects. The soul, mind, and even the heart in its biblical understanding are all spiritual parts of man. A human is neither a body with a spirit, nor is he a spirit with a body. A human is both physical and metaphysical as he has both a body and spirit now and will one day have his spirit united with a glorified body in the new heavens and earth. Some physical creations do not have a spirit, and some spiritual beings do not have a physical nature. How can those with a biblical worldview know that the spiritual nature of creatures is what separates them from other material objects in the universe?

February 12: Soul

The Soul is the metaphysical source of a human being's life and personhood. The words we translate into "soul" in the Bible are *nephesh* in Hebrew and *psuche* in Greek. We use the Greek word to speak of the study of the mind: psychology. However, the modern discipline of psychology stems from a more naturalistic view of man, and, therefore, the goal is typically more about studying brain synapses than a biblical view of who a person is. The soul is often used to speak of the whole being, and not just a spiritual component of man. Because of this, whenever a Christian engages in anthropology, we cannot separate the mere customs of a group from their spiritual nature and well-being. How can Christians treat the whole person as a valuable creature of God?

February 13: Mind

In Scripture, the people of God are commanded to love the Lord God with their mind (Matt. 22:37). *The Mind is the immaterial seat of reasoning and consciousness of the human being.* Because the mind is capable of utilizing both knowledge and wisdom, it can be assumed that both of these areas should have loving God as their goal. The Proverbs tell us that "the fear of the Lord is the beginning of knowledge" (Prov. 1:7). This means to truly understand reality, we must truly know God. Our minds are limited, but, because of the Fall, the mind has also been affected negatively. Although truth can be rightly understood by humanity, we cannot rely on our mental faculties to always be accurate in understanding truth, including the truths of God. How can we renew our minds according to Scripture? *Ref: Mark 12:30; Eph. 4:17–18, 23–32; Rom. 12:2*

February 14: Heart

In addition to being a physical organ, *the Heart is the immaterial seat of the will and emotions of a human being.* Although, in our modern context, we put a lot of focus on what our heart desires, the heart is wicked and deceitful according to Scripture, (Jer. 17:9), and, therefore, we tend to desire the wrong things in life. In addition, we can harden our hearts to the things of God. Because we ought to love the Lord God with all our heart, it is important that both our desires and our emotions are rightfully oriented with God. If we are with God, we should not worry (Matt. 6:25–34), but instead, have righteous sorrow, zeal, indignation (2 Cor. 7:9–11), and joy (John 15:11). How can we make sure we guard our hearts as Christians? *Ref.: Ps. 95:7–11; Prov. 4:23; Jer. 17:9; Heb. 3:7–19*

February 15: Will

The Will of a person is the part of them that acts based on their condition and the conditions around them. Because humanity existed in innocence before the Fall, in sin after the Fall, and in the Holy Spirit once a person becomes a Christian, there are many factors to consider in looking at a mankind's will. Before the Fall, it seems that humanity was able to act in total freedom apart from the introduction of knowledge of good and evil. After the Fall, sin entered humanity and negatively affected the whole of the person. This makes it so that our will does not always want what is good. But, through the Holy Spirit, Christians can act in accordance with the will of God. The persons of the Trinity are the only persons with perfect wills, as they cannot act sinfully. How can Christians make good or bad decisions in this fallen world? *Ref. Gen. 2:17; Rom. 12:1–2*

February 16: Conscience

A human's Conscience is the part of the person that can reflect upon themselves, often responding with a sense of guilt. When the prophet Nathan confronted David about his sin with Bathsheba, David prayed for a clean heart (Ps. 51:10). In the New Testament, Paul speaks quite a bit about not harming someone else's conscience in 1 Corinthians, and having a pure conscience in the Pastoral Epistles. We can even go so far in our sin that we can sear our conscience (1 Tim. 4:2). It is important to remember that our conscience is a part of our humanity, as we have God's Law written on our heart and respond to objective morality (Rom. 2:15). If the believing person has Christ's righteousness (Rom. 3:22), how can we have comfort when our conscience reminds us of past sins? *Ref.: 1 Cor. 8:7–12; 10:25–29; 1 Tim. 1:19; Titus 1:15*

February 17: Knowledge

Knowledge is the acquisition of information. This information can be true or not. Certain information can be made secretive or known only to a small group. A group called the Gnostics, named after a Greek word for knowledge (*gnosis*), began forming during the NT and later created their own false scriptures claiming to know secret information about God. Although we read in the Bible that knowledge can lead to arrogance (1 Cor. 8:1–2), is important that we are not anti-intellectual. God, creating us in His image, gave us the ability to know in a limited degree based in His all-knowing attribute. While we can only learn so much information in our lifetime, God knows all things that are true. How can we make sure that we learn truth and avoid falsehood?

February 18: Wisdom

Unlike a lot of creation, we know that humanity has both sentience, or empirical understanding, and sapience, which is experiential or wise understanding. *Wisdom is knowledge, often experiential, based in good discernment.* Philosophy is the love (*philos*) of wisdom (*sophia*). A proverb is an encapsulation of wisdom in a saying or aphorism. Solomon wrote his son a book of Proverbs that is an inspired collection of wise sayings that we have as Scripture today. Here, we are told that "the fear of the Lord is the beginning of wisdom" (Prov. 9:10). Wisdom is contrasted with foolishness and often figured out through long fought lessons of life in trial and error. For this reason, young people are typically better off learning wisdom from elders early rather than learning from old, difficult lessons.

February 19: Flesh

It is obvious that human beings have bodies. Our bodies can only last so long on this earth, as they are subject to failure due to the Fall. The term flesh (*sarx* in Greek) can also refer to individual people and mankind. But when Scripture speaks of the flesh, it does so in some theological ways, as well. In the Bible, *the Flesh is the physical part of man and the part that is often associated with sin.* The phrase "in the flesh" or "of the flesh" is a term that gets repeated in the New Testament, and it is almost always speaking of how Christians can act apart from the Holy Spirit. It is important to know that Christians are able to act from both a Spiritual and a fleshly source because we can often act inconsistently with what we believe. How can we as Christians make sure that we live from a Spiritual position and not from our condition in the flesh?

February 20: Bipartite

Does humanity have two aspects of our nature or three? There is a debate in the church as to which of these views is more biblical. The term *Bipartite is the belief that human beings are made of two things: soul and body.* Like many of the terms for the different components of mankind, the terms soul and spirit are often used interchangeably in the Scriptures. Some have argued that if this is the case, then maybe they are synonyms for the same idea. The simple framing of an immaterial part and a physical part of who humanity is would fit well with the dualism that the Christian worldview holds to. Then again, what would we do with all of the verses that seem to separate these two ideas? *Ref.: Matt. 10:28; 1 Cor. 5:3; 3 John 2*

February 21: Tripartite

In the debate of whether we are made up of two aspects or three, it may seem obvious that being made of one physical part and one metaphysical part would fit with the concept of Christian dualism. But there are faithful sects of Christianity that have historically held to man having three parts. The term *Tripartite is the belief that human beings are made of three things: spirit, soul, and body.* First of all, although the terms soul and spirit seem interchangeable in many passages in the Bible, they are separate terms in both the Old and New Testaments. There is also the distinction that both animals and humans have souls but only mankind has a spirit. Then there are passages which speak of both the soul and spirit as separate parts. In some Christian sects, they say that this fits with the concept of the Trinity. Which belief do you hold and why? *Ref.: 1 Thess 5:23; Heb. 4:12*

February 22: Race

Race is the arbitrary classification of humans into groups based off of ancestral origin and external characteristics like skin pigment. Race as a term was popularized by Charles Darwin in his works *The Descent of Man*, and *On Origin of the Species…* which includes the term *…Favored Races…* in its longer title. The term "race" is an issue because it cannot fit into domain, kingdom, phylum, class, order, family, genius, or species. It seems more like a subspecies, but that would be dividing homo sapiens. This concept has led to prejudice from both Christians and non-Christians alike, but Darwinism has led to more justification for racism in our modern context. If Scripture uses tribes, tongues, and nations for human groups, should we instead use race?

February 23: Gender

Gender is the classification of human beings into male and female. In the modern period, there has been a move to separate gender, our male-ness or female-ness, and sex, which is our gendered anatomy and chromosomes. But what would the need be for this separation? There is no scientific need to separate these two concepts. Since the formulation of ideologies that are reactionary towards western philosophy, many have sought to counter Middle Eastern and Western Christian influence with reactionary, largely German philosophy, like the works of Karl Marx, to make reality claims about power. However, in the Bible, the description of biology and the commands by God for ordered society is not a power play but recognition of natural and supernatural truth. How can Christians value scriptural masculinity and femininity?

February 24: Transhumanism

Evolutionary theory has been the dominant cultural view of speciation. This has influenced people to desire to speed up the process for human advancement. *Transhumanism is the artificial evolution of a human using technology.* Transhumanism can be as simple as replacing body parts with artificial ones to consolidating all of one's collective data online to make a virtual self. As an intentional movement, some have sought to use body modification to improve their capabilities and life spans. Transhumanism is of interest to biblical anthropology because of the impact of rapid technological advancement on the human person. How do Christians navigate the use of technology to advance the Gospel while also respecting God's creation and our bodies as a temple of God?

February 25: Abortion

Abortion is the practice of medically miscarrying a human in utero. Abortion has been a eugenic practice throughout history. Because many are involved in human pregnancy, the debate over when life begins and who decides in the process has been a tension point in modern politics. Rare yet realized situations, like the death of the mother or pregnancies caused by rape, have often been concerns of one side in political engagement, while issues like its nature as murder and the amount performed are issues discussed by the other. Thomas Aquinas held a view that life began at some point in the womb because Scripture speaks of God knowing (Jer. 1:5) and knitting us in the womb (Ps. 139:13–16), but most Christians today believe life begins at conception. With this in mind, how can Christians engage well in this debate?

February 26: "I and Thou"

When we live our lives, we come across many objects that we interact with. These are called "I-It" relationships. But what happens when we interact with other persons? *The "I-Thou" relationship is the personal experience of other personal experiences, as opposed to the "I-It" relationship of interacting with an object.* This idea was developed by Jewish theologian Martin Buber, and was adopted by some Christian theologians. These thinkers valued personal experience over objective reality. And while it is of vital importance for the Christian to understand that God exists whether someone knows Him or not, is there also something valuable about personal interaction with not only people, but God as well?

February 27: Animism

When finding the default worldview of humanity, it is a universal phenomenon that mankind holds the view of animism. *Animism is the belief that all objects have spirits which are subject to fear and manipulation.* In Romans 1:16–25, Paul tells us that all humanity can recognize the wrath, power, and godhead of God. He also states that we worship the creation rather than the creator. That is, people know there is a God but attribute His reality to natural objects. Because these spirits can be both negative and positive, it is a common practice to develop rituals of manipulation around negative spirits for safety and positive spirits for gain. If Christianity is true, these spirits are at best non-existent and at worst demons. The church has often gone to animistic groups to teach them the gospel, read and write in their language, and meet material needs.

February 28: Naturalism

Naturalism is the worldview that believes the only thing that is real is the physical world. There are many that presume that naturalism is the default view of man because we are born ignorant of the Judeo-Christian God. Yet, this cannot be because people, by default, seem to know there is something supernatural out there to satisfy meaning, just like we understand there is food to satisfy hunger. Consistent naturalists tend not to believe in the reality of metaphysical truths, like shapes, numbers, and concepts like morality. They also believe all matter is equal. One form of naturalism, called "humanism," holds the arbitrary view that humans are somehow important in the universe, and, therefore, require more dignity than the rest of the cosmos.

February 29: New Age Spirituality

New Age Spirituality is a Westernized version of Eastern religion that sees the self as most important. In Eastern religions like Hinduism and Buddhism, man is god in the sense that everything in the cosmos is god (which is called Pantheism), man is part of that everything, and, therefore, man is god. In the New Age view, man is god in that the self is all that truly exists (also called solipsism), or that others might exist, and man can understand true reality through altered consciousness. This can be done through psychedelics, occult practices, or through using Eastern beliefs to manifest reality. New Age Spirituality has increased in popularity since the 1990's and is therefore relevant for biblical anthropology to wrestle with as a powerful view of the self that is contrary to Scripture.

March: God the Father

March 1: Theology Proper

Theology Proper is the study of the nature and attributes of God, and more specifically, about God the Father. Because the term "god" can be used to speak of everything from very limited polytheistic deities to all things being "god," it is helpful to define what we mean when we speak of the God of the Bible. It is important to remember that when we learn about God, we cannot be exhaustive in our understanding of Him. Because we are finite and He is infinite in His attributes, we could study who He is into eternity and never completely comprehend Him. But it is fair to say that He gave us His Word to understand Him to the degree that we need to. How do you learn more about God?

March 2: Deism

Deism is the belief that there is one impersonal god who is not involved with the cosmos it created. During the Enlightenment (1600s to 1800s), some in Western philosophy began to minimize the attributes and works of the God of their Christian heritage due to their current understanding of the sciences. They believed God created but has no other involvement in the cosmos. This is why, although there are many references to God in the early American documents, there is no reference to Jesus, as it was a compromise among the Christian, Deist, and Quaker beliefs of the Founding Fathers. Modern deism can come in a form where post-Christian people who know of and pray to God when they need Him are, otherwise, irreligious and do not meet together in worship. How can we know God is personal?

March 3: Names of God

The various Names of God in Scripture demonstrate God's personhood and attributes, and we often see them after events. In addition to *Adonai* (Lord), there are *El(ohim)* (God) names and *Yahweh* names: *El Elyon* (Most High God) (Gen. 14:18); *El Roi* (God Sees) (Gen. 16:13); *El Shaddai* (God Almighty) (Gen. 17:1); *El Olam* (God Everlasting) (Gen. 21:33); *Yahweh Jireh* (Yahweh Provides) (Gen. 22:14); *Yahweh Raah* (Yahweh Shepherd) (Gen. 48:15); *Yahweh Rapha* (Yahweh Heals) (Exod 15:26); *Yahweh Nissi* (Yahweh our Banner) (Exod. 17:15); *Yahweh Mekoddishkem* (Yahweh Sanctifies) (Exod. 31:13); *Yahweh Shalom* (Yahweh is Peace) (Judg. 6:24); *Yahweh Sabaoth* (Yahweh of Hosts) (1 Sam. 1:3); *Yahweh Tsidkenu* (Yahweh Righteousness) (Jer. 23:6); and *Yahweh Shammah* (Yahweh is There) (Ezek. 48:35).

March 4: Unity

When we read passages like the Shema in Deuteronomy 6:4, we see that ancient Israelites held the view that there was only one God. *The Unity of God is the idea that there is only one God according to Scripture.* The belief in this view is known as monotheism, and it stands in contrast to the common ancient belief of multiple gods, called polytheism. The monotheistic religions of Judaism and Islam are strictly *Unitarian*, which is *the belief that there is one god who is one person*. But Christianity holds the belief in one God and three persons. Because God is one, when we discuss the various attributes of God, these can be understood as describing the Father, the Son, and the Holy Spirit. How can our worship reflect our belief in one God?

March 5: Trinity

The Trinity is the doctrine that teaches the Christian deity is one God and three persons: the Father, the Son, and the Holy Spirit. This doctrine is often taught by stating the Father is neither the Son nor the Holy Spirit, the Son is neither the Father nor the Holy Spirit, and the Holy Spirit is neither the Father nor Son, but they are all God. Ideas like *Tritheism*, that teaches *there are three gods*, or *modalism/Sabellianism*, that teach *there is one god that takes on three modes or representations*, are therefore heretical views. This view is important because although we see God as a singular being in the Old Testament, we are introduced to the persons of the Son and Holy Spirit in the New Testament. How are the three persons seen as distinct at Jesus' baptism (Matt. 3:13–17; Mark 1:9–11; Luke 3:21–22) and in the Great Commission (Matt. 28:19)?

March 6: Omniscience

Omniscience is the doctrine stating that God knows all truth. Christians debate whether God can know potentials that do not occur, but it is agreed that God knowing all truth is important. First, a God who cannot know all things cannot produce a flawless Scripture. Secondly, end times events are often explained in Scripture to motivate the followers of God that He will ultimately be victorious, but this entire genre of literature could be called into question due to its uncertainty. Even Christ's work on the cross cannot be guaranteed if God cannot know its long-term results. On the contrary, if God knows all truth, He is aware of all of our thoughts, as well as all our past and future actions. How can we worship God for His omniscience? *Ref.: Job 21:22; Heb. 4:13*

March 7: Omnipotence

Omnipotence is the doctrine that claims God is all powerful. God's omnipotence is necessary mainly because God can then be sovereign over all creation. God's omnipotence also makes prayer for God's intervention with our future possible. Also, God's being all powerful is important because it differentiates Him from every non-monotheistic religion. The larger the pantheon, the more separated godly power would be. Even views that claim their god is all things or in all things do not have an all-powerful god because it would merely practice self-control. God's power over all can be seen in Him creating, but also in His sustaining and manipulation of creation in His miraculous works. Conceptual reality is also not more powerful than God because concepts have been thought by God before creation. How can we worship an all-powerful God?

March 8: Omnipresence

Omnipresence is the doctrine that teaches God is present at all places at once. God is not omnipresent because He is spiritual. Angelic beings are also spiritual beings, but they have locality in their spirit, even if multiple angels could occupy the same space at the same time. God is present everywhere because His presence is not limited. The one place separated from God seems to be Hell. But this is not because God cannot go there, as God created Hell and is over it. It is because that is where people who are separated from God remain. God's omnipresence is important because we can know God cannot be excluded from a location. For the believer, the Holy Spirit can indwell a believer and be wherever they are. How can we worship an omnipresent God? *Ref.: Jer. 23:23–24; Matt. 6:6*

March 9: Immateriality

God's Immateriality is the doctrine that tells us God is not made of matter. God is not an abstract object, like a concept, but a spiritual, concreate object who is personal. Because God is spiritual, He is also immaterial. God cannot be material because the Creator of all matter and time cannot be made of His material or temporal creation. Matter is also spatially located, meaning, if God is omnipresent, He cannot be material. Because God is immaterial, God is also invisible, as well (Col. 1:15). Because of God's immateriality, there is also a "hiddenness" that God has. This results in some claiming that this is a negative attribute, arguing if God is hidden, we cannot fault people for not believing in Him. But God's immateriality does not equate to His not existing or that He has not shown Himself. How has God shown who He is without needing materiality?

March 10: Transcendence

God often seems unrelatable to us because we are fallible and limited and He is infallible and unlimited in His attributes. This is because God is transcendent. *Transcendence is the belief that God is far off from humanity.* God's being maximally great can cause a sense of wonder and joy as well as fear and finality. Apart from God's otherworldly attributes, God's distance from us can also be seen in the holiness of ritual cleansing in the sacrificial system of the Mosaic Law. Because God is known to humanity intrinsically (Rom. 1:18–32), it is worthwhile for people to contemplate God's overwhelming greatness (Ps. 8:4), as God requests that we be holy as He is holy (Lev. 21:8; 1 Pet. 1:16). How can we meditate on God's transcendence and worship Him in awe?

March 11: Immanence

Even though God is grand and wonderful in His transcendence, He is also close to humanity, as well. This is because God is imminent. *Immanence is the belief that God is near to humanity.* The obvious demonstration of God's relatability to mankind is the fact that the second person of the Trinity took on humanity to be known as the God-man Jesus of Nazareth. In this way, we understand that Jesus knows what it is like to be truly human. But God is imminent in more ways than the Son's incarnation. God's creating us in His likeness relates mankind directly to Himself. Although our initial relationship with God in our innocence was close in the garden, believers have the Holy Spirit indwell them at all times, as we are even called the Temple (1 Cor. 3:16–17; 2 Cor. 6:16). Also, we will one day be closer to Him in heaven. How can we worship an imminent God?

March 12: Aseity

Aseity is the doctrine that speaks of God's self-existence. Genesis 1 speaks of God's existence before creation, but the articulation of aseity goes back to Aristotle's prime mover argument. Because the universe breaks down in entropy, we know it cannot have existed infinitely into the past. There had to be something not made of the cosmos that created the cosmos. God is immaterial and timeless, so He qualifies as the one who could create the cosmos. The same idea is the basis for God's self-existence. Because something cannot make itself, God is not His own creator. Because God is good and powerful, and it would neither be good nor powerful to not exist, God must exist. How can we worship God in His self-existence?

March 13: Necessity

Necessity is the doctrine that argues God must exist. Nothing that we know in the cosmos must exist or be the way it is. In fact, the one thing that is necessary in the cosmos is that the created world needs a Creator. If you can think of any physical object including creatures, there could be many different ways that object could be different or even not exist. The same could be said about timelines and events. There is even a possibility that matter or time could never have existed. But the same cannot be said of God. There are concepts like numbers that would seem to exist even if there was nothing to count or people to count them. But it is odd that this is the case. This means there is a being that must exist to ground this and other concepts. All of this points to the need for God's existence. How can we worship a God that must exist?

March 14: Eternity

Eternity is the doctrine that teaches God is outside of time. Another way to speak of this idea is whether or not something is temporal (having to do with time) or atemporal (having to do without time). When scientists study the known universe, they can only go back to T=1, where the symbol "T" is "time." This is because T=0 would be like how things were before we had matter and time, and we cannot use the scientific method to test what things were like without matter and time. God not only exists before time began, but many theologians argue God is outside time altogether. One way that we know God is eternal is because Jesus states, "before Abraham was, I am" (John 8:58). Because of our limitation to time, it is difficult for us to grasp God's relationship to events that happen within time. How is God's eternality a comfort to you?

March 15: Infinity

Infinity is the doctrine that speaks of God's being limitless. Because we are part of the closed system of everything that God has created, we are as limited as the rest of creation in every way. But God is separate from the created order, and, therefore, He is limitless. We are limited in space, time, character, and output, whereas God is spaceless, timeless, perfect, and powerful. Physical and temporal reality are limited, but so are abstract objects like shapes and numbers. An interesting consideration is that, although infinity can be understood using mathematics like calculus, infinity can also show math to have limits, like the results of infinity subtracted from itself. Infinity is grounded in God, not mathematics. How can we worship a limitless God?

March 16: Immutability

Immutability is the doctrine that argues God is unchanging. God cannot change because that is inconsistent with His being and attributes. If we can definitively say He is all good and all powerful, He cannot change because He could then cease to be those things. God's immutability extends to His inability to lie as He cannot change His promises (Heb. 6:17–18). This aspect of His unchanging nature is helpful to consider when reading about prophecies and God's covenants. One could argue the Son's incarnation is God's changing. This is not His deity changing, though, but the adding a human nature to one person in the Trinity. God's immutability is a comfort to Christians, because, in a cosmos that is constantly changing in some way or another, there is a genuinely reliable constant that humanity can hold onto. How can we worship God in His immutability?

March 17: Impassibility

Impassibility is the doctrine that states God does not have passion. God's not having passion relates to both God's immutability and His inability to be harmed. Because of this, any passage in Scripture that describes God with emotional language is merely using personification, or ascribing human qualities for non-human things. For example, when the Bible speaks of God's repentance in passages like Genesis 6:6, we can understand this as the author speaking of God's actions from a human perspective. This doctrine is not seen in the human suffering of the God-Man Jesus Christ, for example, through His suffering in being beaten and hung on the cross. Although it is difficult for us to understand as humans who live in a fallen world, how can we worship God in His impassibility?

March 18: Ineffability

Ineffability is the doctrine that speaks of our inability to fully comprehend God. The Bible is a text that exists for us to understand God, and it is obvious that God wants us to know Him to some degree. But problems exist due to our finite nature and God's infinity. For one, the Bible does not express everything about God. So, even if we could fully understand all of the information in Scripture, God would still be ineffable. Also, God, Himself, is by nature infinite, and, therefore, we could not completely understand Him even if all knowledge of Him was available to us. Thankfully, God does not demand or ask that we perfectly understand Him, but only that we know Him. How can we understand God better in order to worship Him well? *Ref.: Job 11:7; Rom. 11:33*

March 19: Immortality

Immortality is the doctrine that teaches God is unending life. Death has both a physical component, in our current life ending, and a spiritual component, in our eternal separation from God. Life can be seen as the opposite of both of these realities. God is the creator and source of all life (Gen. 1), and, because He is unlimited, His life is unlimited. Because God is the source of life, this also extends to His granting eternal life to others, as we see Jesus claiming to be the source of our second life (John 3:16; 14:6). If the Fall introduced both kinds of death, this confirms our separation from the source of life and our need for that life to be repaired in Christ. The condition of this eternal life is based in our belief in Jesus Christ and His offer of reconciliation with the Father. How can we better worship God knowing that He is the immortal source of all life?

March 20: Glory

Glory is the brilliant awe that is sourced in God. In both creation and in the end, all physical sources of light are gone and yet light remains. This is because of God's glory. Because it would result in death, no one has seen God (John 1:18; 1 John 4:12), except for Moses, who was only allowed to see God's glory briefly (Exod. 33:17–23). One way God has shown Himself indirectly has been by theophanies, or representations of God in seemingly physical ways, typically as light. Abraham saw God as a furnace and lamp, Moses saw God as a burning bush and a pillar of smoke and fire, and Daniel saw God's hand writing on a wall, for some examples. God's glory dwelled in the Holy of Holies in the Tabernacle/Temple (Exod. 40:34; 1 Kgs. 8:10–11), although it left in Ezekiel's day (Ezek. 10). How can we worship the God of glory in this life?

March 21: Beauty

Beauty is the aesthetic goodness that is grounded in God's being. Physical things like sunsets or other humans can be beautiful, and so can concepts like love or a series of words like poems. People find many things in this life beautiful, but the question many have is what makes something beautiful? There is a personal aspect to beauty, as not all people find the exact same things beautiful, but the concept of beauty is a universal understanding. Therefore, the concept must be universal. Because beauty could exist without anything to describe as beautiful, it must be grounded in God, who created all. This follows as every beautiful thing that exists was created by God. Therefore, our appreciation of beauty should be in light of God as its source. How can we better worship God in His beauty?

March 22: Holiness

Holiness is the divine purity that separates God from unclean creation. God is holy in His moral and spiritual character. Because God is Holy, there has been a divide between God and mankind since humanity has become sinful after the Fall. Since this time, some pious people have had some positive experiences with God (Isa. 6:1–8). In the Mosaic Law, though, God instituted a ritual process to help man get from unclean to clean and from clean to holy. Because of sin, humanity keeps polluting himself, so the cleanliness and holiness are not permanent. But since the permanent sacrifice of Christ, the holiness of God is able to be permanently given to redeemed mankind through the Holy Spirit who sanctifies us. The book of Hebrews contrasts the OT system with a priesthood of believers in Christ. How can we be holy as God is holy?

March 23: Morality

Morality is what is right and good grounded in the character of God contrasted with what is wrong and evil. Ethics is the study of morality, and what is moral is considered ethical. Christians have a few options of viewing morality. One could see morality as categories of virtues and vices, a series of divine commands from God, or parts of what make up the law of the natural world. Morality cannot be an agreed upon set of rules or opinions about right and wrong, because these views are subjective and not grounded in God. Instead, we know that God is the good (Ps. 34:8; 1 John 4:8), and any good action that we could do or obligation we ought to perform is only good or right if it is consistent with God's character or commands. How can we be godly in morality?

March 24: Righteousness

Righteousness is the perfect character and perspective that God has in judgment. In our society, we see many instances of injustice, or actions that are not the way they should be. When human judges determine whether something is lawful, justice is limited in many ways: in the judge's ignorance of every fact in the case, the judge's inability to make a perfect determination in the case, and even whether or not that law is truly just in nature. But God's justice is perfect. First, God knows all, so He can make decisions with every truth in mind. Also, God can make perfectly right judgments because of His perfect character. For example, when God told Israel to take the land (Deut. 7), He was able to use the imperfect Israelites to carry out justice because He rightly determined the Canaanites needed judgment. How can we worship a righteous God?

March 25: Perfection

Perfection is the attribute of flawlessness that can only be found in God. God is perfect in His being, nature, will, and attributes (Ps. 18:30). Because God is flawless, and we know of God naturally, we are able to gauge different things as how they ought to be based in God's perfection. Even if humanity is fallen, we are able to understand that certain things should be a certain way or not. For a moral example, if someone steals from us, we know that is not how things should be. If we are in pain, we know that is not how we normally ought to be. But God, to be consistent with His limitless attributes, cannot have any flaws. This perfection adds to our experience of God as transcendent. If God is perfect and humanity is not, how can we better worship a perfect God?

March 26: Jealousy

Jealousy, as an attribute of God, *is the protective quality God has regarding His exclusive worship.* In the Scriptures, God is often described as "jealous" regarding His worship (Exod. 20:5; 34:14; Deut. 6:15). This is because God is the only being worthy of worship. Whenever a person worships someone or something other than God, it is wrongly placed and sinful. God is concerned about misplaced worship because our free will ability to worship is not neutral. When we are committed to showing worth to another being or object, we are actively saying that being or object has the right to worth that is God's alone. God is rightfully desirous of the worship that ought to be given to Him. Our relational jealousy for our spouse is an imperfect representation of God's jealousy as we are made in His image. What might you worship that is not God?

March 27: Goodness

Goodness as an attribute of God is the fact that God is love and His lovingkindness is experienced throughout creation. God is love (1 John 4:8, 16), and, therefore, any true show of love is ultimately sourced in God. English translations betray just how many forms of love exist in the Bible. In Hebrew, we translate the words *ahavah* as love, *hesed* as lovingkindness, *raya* as friend/lover, and *dod* as beloved. In Greek, love can be *phileo* or brotherly, *storge* or parental, *eros* or romantic, and *agape* or high love. God's love is typically *hesed* and *agape*. All human love should be Godly even though it is typically selfish. The Godly love that Christians have for one another is sourced in the Holy Spirit that indwells us. How can we love others as God loves?

March 28: Actuality

Actuality is the doctrine that speaks of God's pure existence. The Greek philosopher Aristotle spoke of a being of pure actuality even from a polytheistic worldview. Although there are issues with this concept in the Greco-Roman worldview, from the Bible, we understand that God not only fits the description of a being of pure actuality, but it answers how God does not need a creator and can create from nothing. God is existence, but this does not mean everything that exists is made of God. The creation accounts in the Greek *Theogony* and the Roman *Metamorphosis* have the gods creating out of existing material, including themselves. The God of the Bible is pure being separate from creation, but we as creative beings made by Him cannot create *ex nihilo* like He does. If God is pure existence, how can we worship Him better in our lives?

March 29: Simplicity

Philosophically, it can be asked, "at what point is a thing many parts or a whole?" *Simplicity is the doctrine that argues God is one being without parts.* Even though God can be described as having many attributes that we can speak of separately, God, Himself, is not made out of a series of parts. Even God's being Trinitarian does not disqualify His simplicity because God's being three persons does not mean God is three separate parts. Even though human beings have separate physical organs, and we can speak of humans as having a mind, soul, or spirit, we are each individual persons and not merely the sum of our parts. But God does not even have physical or spiritual components that could be taken away to make Him less God. Therefore, how can we worship God better as we understand God's simplicity?

March 30: Sovereignty

Sovereignty is the doctrine that speaks of God's ruling and reigning above creation. Because God is the Creator of all, He is not equal to it, and, therefore, He is over that creation in superiority. God's kingly authority is seen as the ultimate authority of creation, but He was also the local king of Israel until they requested a physical king (1 Sam. 8). But God is not merely superior to creation, He also sustains creation. We see examples of God's common grace as the Bible speaks of His provision for creatures (Matt. 6:25–32). Although different sects of Christianity debate the extent of God's sovereignty, it is not in question that God is ultimate ruler of the cosmos according to the biblical data (Isa. 41:17–20; Col. 1:16–17), and that His authority will continue to the end (Rev. 22:3–4). How is God king in your life?

March 31: Providence

Providence is the doctrine that speaks of how God brings His will about in created order. Providence, typically understood, argues that God has complete control over all events that take place in creation. But in different theological views, the debate is to what degree God is involved with the actions of created order and whether or not He is permanently involved in all actions or oversees systems that are in place. Regardless of the degree of involvement God may have, there are obvious instances of God's desires coming about. We see, through the existence of prophecy, that whether or not there are possibilities of different ways events can take place, God intends events to end up a certain way. How does God's providence give you comfort in your life?

April: God the Son

April 1: Christology

Christology is the study of Jesus Christ as God the Son and the Savior of humanity. Because Jesus is central to the Christian faith, He, His nature, and His works have been studied by many theologians of many different theological traditions and from many methodologies. Because of this, there is much biblical, traditional, and theological information to sift through when understanding the God-Man Jesus Christ. Getting the Son's existence, person, natures, and works correct can mean the difference of whether one is in right relationship with God or not. It is from this vantage point that one can rightly look at the biblical doctrines and suspect heresies regarding Jesus and determine what is true about the Savior of mankind. Only by examining the Scriptures can we have a right understanding the Son of God. What can you do to get to know Jesus better?

April 2: Low Christology

Low Christology is the focus on the human nature of Jesus when studying the Son. Because Jesus was a fully human male rabbi living in first century Roman Palestine, the material and literary data surrounding His life can be studied. Even though this study is necessary in understanding Jesus, some in skeptical scholarship have put sole focus in this area. Starting in the 1700s, several movements saw the "Historical Jesus" as merely a human, removing any reference to His divinity. And although the idea began in the nineteenth century, there has recently begun a revival of "mythicism," or the belief that Jesus never existed at all, despite almost unanimous agreement in Christian and secular scholarship otherwise. How can we better know the man Jesus but not only as human?

April 3: High Christology

High Christology is the focus on the divine nature of Jesus when studying the Son. The Old Testament does not mention the Son explicitly because theological clarity is only available through progressive revelation after Christ's death, burial, and resurrection. But the authors of the New Testament saw Jesus as the pre-incarnate Son being involved in God's work of creation. Passages like Col. 1:15–19, Heb. 1:2–3, and John 1:1–3 all speak of Jesus as Creator and having authority attributed to God in the Old Testament. All of the attributes of God that are covered in Theology Proper are applicable to the divine nature of the Son. The theological questions regarding Jesus begin when we discuss Low Christology in light of High Christology, but Scripture can give clarity on both natures of Jesus. How can we better know the divine Son Jesus with His humanity?

April 4: Pre-Incarnate Son

The Pre-Incarnate Son was the way the second person of the Trinity was with exclusively divine nature before taking on His human nature. In the OT, this person of the Trinity, the Father, and the Holy Spirit can all be in view when God is referenced as they are indistinguishable in divinity. We do not see explicit references of the Son in the OT, but we do have many implicit references. Visual appearances like the Angel of the Lord and verbal references like the Lord saying to "my Lord" in Psalm 110 are typically understood as appearances or allusions to the Son. Jesus even used the term *ego eimi*, translated "I am" in English, to refer to Himself with the divine name of God YHWH as existing before Abraham (John 8:58). What are examples of the Son in the OT?

April 5: Christophany

A *Christophany is an appearance of the Son in the Old Testament.* In order to understand what a Christophany is, it is helpful to know that a *Theophany is an appearance of God in the Old Testament.* Because no man has seen God, any time God has appeared, people hear things like God's voice (Gen. 2:16–17; Matt. 3:17) or see things like a burning bush (Exod. 3:2–6). Christophanies are typically events where a Theophany occurs, but there seems to be a bodily manifestation of God or God is interacting with God in the Old Testament. When the Angel of the Lord wrestles with Jacob (Gen. 32:22–32), the fourth "son of the gods" appears with Daniel's friends in the furnace (Dan. 3:24–26), and when God speaks to the Lord in the Psalms (Ps. 110), these may all be OT appearances of the Son. How can we determine when Christophanies occur?

April 6: Angel of the Lord

The Angel of the Lord is often considered a pre-incarnate Christophany that appears throughout the Old Testament. The Angel of the Lord appears to Hagar (Gen. 16:7–11), Abraham (Gen. 22:11–15), Moses (Exod. 3:2), Balaam (Num. 22:22–35), the Israelites, Gideon, and Samson's Parents in Judges (Judg. 2:1–4; 6:11–22; 13:3–21), David (1 Chr. 21:12–30), Elijah (1 Kgs. 19:7; 2 Kgs. 1:3, 15; 19:35), and Zechariah (Zech. 1:11–14; 3:1–6; 12:8). The Angel of the Lord seems to be militaristic (Pss. 34:7; 35:5–6; 1 Chr. 21:12–30) which could make him the "Commander of the Lord's Army" in Joshua (Josh. 5:13–15), who accepts worship, as the Angel of the Lord also does (Judg. 6:11–22; 13:3–21). If the Angel of the Lord were not the pre-incarnate Son, how could we determine who it could be?

April 7: Messianic Prophecies

Messianic Prophecies are prophecies that are given throughout the Old Testament that speak of the future Messiah and what He will do. The OT has many verses that speak of a coming Messiah. To provide only a few of the numerous prophecies regarding Jesus in the Old Testament: Jesus will be born of a virgin (Gen. 3:15; Isa. 7:14) in Bethlehem (Mic. 5:2) as a Jewish man (Gen. 22:18) in the line of Judah (Gen. 49:10) through the Royal line of David (Isa. 11:1; Jer. 23:5), that He would suffer and die (Ps. 22; Isa. 50:6; 53:5, 7), resurrect (Ps. 16:10), and ascend to the right hand of God (Ps. 110:1). There are many times where Jesus set out to fulfill prophecies (Matt. 13:14; Luke 4:21; John 15:25), but many were fulfilled around Him (Matt. 2:15, 23; 27:9). How can we worship Jesus better knowing even some of the ways He and His ministry were prophesied?

April 8: Incarnation

The Incarnation is the doctrine that speaks of the Son of God's taking on a human nature. The main thing to know about the incarnation is that, although the Son always existed, the Son has not always had two natures (John 1:14; Gal. 4:4–5; Heb. 1:1–2). The reason that the Son took on a human nature was ultimately to redeem mankind. God cannot die for human sin, and a mere human being cannot save all of mankind through death or in any other way. Therefore, the Son was born fully man through the virgin Mary by Godly miracle as Jesus, God with us ("Immanuel," Isa. 7:14; Matt. 1:23). It is because of this that Jesus can identify with us as human beings, and, as such, Jesus maintains this incarnate nature in glory. How can you better worship the incarnate Son?

April 9: Virgin Birth

The Virgin Birth is the doctrine that states that Mary did not have intimate relations with Joseph to conceive Jesus, but that she was a virgin, and Jesus' conception was a Godly miracle. This is not to be confused with the Roman Catholic doctrine of the *Immaculate Conception, the belief that the Virgin Mary was miraculously born sinless*, because Catholics have held that sin is passed on through propagation. The virgin birth was prophesied in the OT (Isa.7:14), and it is important in considering Jesus' two natures. The Council of Ephesus (431) argued whether Mary was the *Christotokos* (mother of the Messiah), held by those who believed Jesus was two persons, or the *Theotokos* (mother of God), held by those who believed Jesus had two natures, with Theotokos winning out. How does knowing Jesus' birth help you better understand Him?

April 10: Divine Nature

The Divine Nature of the Son is the Godly one of Jesus' two natures. Every attribute of God covered in theology proper is true of the divine nature of the God-man Jesus Christ, and, therefore, He is worthy of our praise and worship in who He is alone. This is important to us because He would not be able to accomplish anything eternal or of power for mankind if He were not God. There were some specific Christological heresies that denied Jesus' deity. *Ebionism was a belief from the second century that denied Jesus' deity and preexistence. Arianism was the fourth century belief that Jesus was not God but the highest creature.* Jesus' divinity was affirmed at the Council of Nicea (AD 325). How can you worship Jesus better considering His divine nature?

April 11: Human Nature

The Human Nature of the Son is the incarnate one of Jesus' two natures. God cannot die, and, therefore, resurrect or ascend bodily, let alone identify with mankind. But Jesus Christ, in His human nature, is as fully human as all of mankind. If Jesus did not have a human nature, none of the work that He accomplished would translate to mankind, if any of it would be possible to be accomplished. There are some christological heresies that denied or limited Jesus' humanity. *Docetism was the first century belief that Jesus only appeared human. Apollinarianism was a fourth century belief that Jesus' human nature had a divine mind. Monophysitism is the view that Jesus had one divine nature.* Although some might have believed that Jesus' having a human nature made Him less worthy of worship, how does Jesus' human nature help you worship Him more?

April 12: Hypostatic Union

The Hypostatic Union is the belief that Jesus Christ is one person who has both a fully human and a fully divine nature. We cannot think of Jesus like a Greek demigod, where He is half god and half man. That would make both natures incomplete, and He, therefore, could not completely identify as one or the other but a new thing. There are some heresies that have existed that confuse Jesus' natures. *Nestorianism was the fifth century view that Jesus was two persons, divine and human. Eutychianism was the fifth century view that Jesus had a drop of humanity in a sea of divinity. Miaphysitism*, the current view of the Oriental Church, *believes that Jesus has one combined human and divine nature.* Why would Jesus' being fully man and fully God in the hypostatic union be important for our salvation?

April 13: Uniqueness

The Uniqueness of the Son is the doctrine that speaks of Jesus as the only true Son of God who can be God, perfectly demonstrate God, and save mankind as the God-man. The idea in the New Testament that refers to Jesus' unique status is His being "only begotten" (*monogenes*). John uses this term for Jesus (John 1:14; 3:16), not speaking of His being created, but of Jesus being uniquely the Son of God. But Jesus cannot be the only son if there are "sons of God" who became this way through salvation (John 1:12). Hebrews solves this dilemma by speaking of Isaac as Abraham's "only begotten" son when Ishmael predated Isaac (Heb. 11:17). This shows that this term is speaking of a special, unique son, and that those that believe in the only begotten Son are not unique in that way. How can we worship Jesus as God's unique Son?

April 14: Kenosis

The Kenosis is the doctrine that teaches the Son "emptied" Himself in the incarnation. The one passage in question is not clear in what is meant by kenosis (Phil. 2:6–7), so there have been many views on this doctrine, some of which are heretical. For example, suggesting the losing or lessening of Jesus' divine nature would be a problem, as He must be fully God. Also, increasing His human nature would not work because He is already fully human. Instead, theologians suggest that Jesus taking on a human nature would seemingly "limit" the Son by making Him not only divine. In this way, Jesus is not limited, His human nature is affirmed, and His human nature is understood as added in time. How can we better worship the Son in His kenosis?

April 15: Sinlessness

The Sinlessness, or impeccability, of Jesus is the doctrine that speaks of Jesus' lack of sin or a sin nature. Although any Christian who is orthodox in their theology would argue that Jesus never sinned, there is a debate as to whether or not Jesus had the ability to sin. One view, those that believe Jesus had peccability, argue that His human nature had the ability to sin, but that He never sinned. This would see passages like Heb. 2:17 and 4:15 say that Jesus would fully know what it would be like to be a fallen human, tempted by His sin nature, yet not sinning. The other view, those seeing Jesus is impeccable, argues that Jesus was fully human, but, having an unfallen human nature, could not actually sin. This balances passages like Heb. 4:15 and 2 Co. 5:21, and would not have the issue of arguing God could sin. How do you view Jesus' sinlessness?

April 16: Messiah

The Messiah is the anticipated "anointed one" of Israel who will bring peace and rule the nations. The terms "messiah" in the OT and "Christ" in the NT both mean "anointed one." In the OT, anointing was a process of pouring or rubbing oil on and by priests and kings commanded by God (1 Sam. 10:1; 2 Sam. 2:4). In the prophets, we start to see the Anointed One as a person that would be king and reverse the wrongs of Israel (Hab. 3:13; Dan. 9:25–26). In the NT, Jesus is called the Christ as the one anticipated in the OT. Luke states that Jesus was anointed by the Holy Spirit (Acts 10:38), but the only times we see Jesus physically anointed are by women, not priests (Luke 7:36–50; John 12:2–8). How can we better worship Jesus knowing He is the Messiah?

April 17: Suffering Servant

The Suffering Servant was an Old Testament prophecy, to be fulfilled in Jesus, of a Ruler who will judge yet experience much pain. These prophecies are in the form of "Servant Songs" in the book of Isaiah (Isa. 42:1–9; 49:1–6; 50:4–9; 52:13—53:12), with similar themes elsewhere in the Old Testament (Ps. 22; Zech. 11:13; 12:10; 13:7). Strong revolutionaries like Judas Maccabees in the intertestamental period flavored a view of the coming Messiah, so that, by the time of the New Testament, the Messiah was expected to overthrow the Roman oppressors. But Jesus demonstrated vulnerability in His life and ultimate death on the cross that fulfilled much of Isaiah's songs (Matt. 26:67; 27:12, 26, 57–60; Luke 22:63; John 15:25) with the rest fulfilled in the end times. How can you better worship the Suffering Servant Jesus Christ?

April 18: Son of God

The Son of God is the title of Jesus Christ that speaks of His divine position compared to the Father. When Christians speak about the Son of God, we often speak about Jesus' place in the Trinity (Matt. 28:19). But the Son of God title reaches back to the OT, with the appearance of the man in the furnace to Daniel's three friends (Dan. 3:25). Jesus often speaks of God as His Father (Matt. 10:32–33), and the Father speaks of Jesus as His Son (Mark 1:11). It is this title that seems to be at the center of the Jews' charge of Jesus committing blasphemy (Matt. 27:40, 43; John 19:7). This title is also at the heart of John's Gospel when he states his purpose in what he wants people to believe about Jesus (John 20:31). How can we better worship Jesus the Son of God?

April 19: Son of Man

The Son of Man is the title of Jesus Christ that speaks of His being the eternal Son incarnate. To our ears, a person saying that they are a "son of man" would be so obvious that it would not need to be mentioned. But for Jesus, this name held much theological meaning. Like "the Son of God," this title dates back to the book of Daniel, referring to a man coming from the clouds to meet God (Dan. 7:13). Jesus' audience would be familiar with this passage, and it would come to their mind when Jesus used this title. In the New Testament, we see that Jesus uses this title of Himself more than any other, appearing about 80 times in the Gospels. The idea for this name seems to indicate both that Jesus is God, and that He came as a human, which was not expected in their understanding of God or the Messiah. How can you better worship Jesus the Son of Man?

April 20: Logos

Although the word *logos* is the Greek term for "word" and "reason," theologically, *Logos is the title of Jesus that indicates His being the ultimate revelation from God.* Firstly, John's usage of the Logos is a reference to Genesis's description of God speaking things into existence "in the beginning," alluding to Jesus' role in creation. Secondly, the idea of the Logos speaks of God's revelation to mankind, previously through the Scriptures but now through God Himself in a tangible form. Whereas a text can be misunderstood or taken out of context, the source of that information can clarify information not only through speaking but in demonstration. How can we better worship the Logos who was in the beginning, is with God, is God (John 1:1), and entered into flesh as Jesus of Nazareth?

April 21: Trilemma

The Trilemma is an argument that states that Jesus is either liar, lunatic, or Lord. The famous apologist C. S. Lewis put forth the trilemma as a three-part problem for those who think of Jesus as just being a good teacher if He claimed to be God. If Jesus claimed to be God, He could have been a liar. The problem with this view is that one would have to demonstrate how a good teacher lies, and how faithful Jews died believing in His deity, miracles, and that He rose from the dead. Jesus could also have been a lunatic thinking He was God, but the same problems arise, not only with His followers being fooled, but with Jesus being fooled as well. The last potential is that Jesus is who He said He was (*kurios*, "Lord"), and we would then only have to wrestle with our own skeptical worldviews. How can we better worship the Lord Jesus Christ?

April 22: Threefold Office

The Threefold Office of Jesus Christ is that He is the ultimate Prophet, Priest, and King. Jesus preexisted these offices, so they can be seen as having Jesus as their archetype. As the Prophet (Deut. 18:15, 18; Acts 3:22; 7:37; Rev. 19:10), Jesus' power as God is seen through miracles (John 9:1–41) and in foretelling what is to come in blessing (Matt. 5:3–11) and judgment (Matt. 23:13–36). As the Priest (Heb. 4:14), Jesus' ministry of redemption is seen in His being the final sacrifice (Heb. 10:4, 10) and being the ultimate high priest (Ps. 110:4; Heb. 7:23–24). As the King (Rev. 17:14; 19:16), Jesus' royal ministry is seen in His ruling (Matt. 19:28; 28:18) and reigning (Rev. 20:4; 22:1, 3). How can we better worship the ultimate Prophet, Priest, and King?

April 23: Discourses of Jesus

The Discourses of Jesus are various long-form teachings of Jesus to groups or individuals. There are many of Jesus' discourses in the Gospels, but the most prominent are the five discourses in Matthew. These are the Sermon on the Mount/Plain (Matt. 5–7; Luke 6:20–49), the Little Commission (Matt. 10), the Parable Discourse (Matt. 13), the Discourse on the Church (Matt. 16–18), and the Olivet Discourse (Matt. 24–25). In John, other discourses are provided (John 6; 8; 10; 14–17), with two important discourses to individuals: a wealthy Jewish man of high social standing (John 3), and a Samaritan woman who has been with many men (John 4). In all of these teachings, we see Jesus speak on how to live presently and in the End often through metaphors and parables. Seeing Jesus' value on teaching truth, how can take Jesus' teachings to others?

April 24: Parables of Jesus

The Parables of Jesus are the many examples of Jesus' teachings through metaphors in the Gospels. Jesus' parables can be for instruction (Matt. 13:1–8), mission (Luke 7:41–43), or the future (Matt. 22:1–14). They can be about the kingdom (Mark 4:30–32), serving others (Matt. 25:13–30), prayer, (Luke 18:1–8), and judgment (Matt. 18:23–35). The "lost" parables (Luke 15:3–32) speak of Jesus' heart for those who need repentance. The rich man and Lazarus (Luke 16:19–31), is the only parable with a real named person, and it shows some insight on first century Israel's understanding of the afterlife. How can you understand Jesus better through His parables? *Ref.: Matt. 13:24–33, 44–50, 52; 20:1–16; 21:28–46; 24:45–51; 25:1–13; Mark 4:26–29; 13:34–37; Luke 10:30–37; 11:5–8; 13:6–9; 14:16; 16:1–10; 17:7–10; 18:9–14; 19:11–27*

April 25: Miracles of Jesus

The Miracles of Jesus are signs, powers, and wonders that He performs to demonstrate His authority as Messiah and God. Jesus heals: a nobleman's son, Peter's mother-in-law, eleven lepers, a paralytic, an infirmed man, a withered hand, centurion's servant, woman with blood, two blind men, many in Gennesaret, a gentile woman's daughter, deaf mute, blind paralytic, an epileptic, man born blind, infirmed woman, man with dropsy, two blind men, restoring ear, and multitude; He resurrects: widow's son, ruler's daughter, and Lazarus; He manipulates nature: water to wine, escaping multitude, calming sea, feeding four and five thousand, walking on sea, and withering a tree; has fish caught: draught of fish, tax from fish's mouth, and a catch of fish; and performs exorcisms: an unclean spirit, from two blind mutes, many into pigs, and from a deaf mute.

April 26: Metaphors for Jesus in New Testament

The various Metaphors for Jesus in the New Testament speak of Jesus' attributes and relationships to humanity and the church. In the Gospels, Jesus is necessary as the Bread of Life (John 6:35), the way humanity can be saved as the Light of the World (John 8:12), the Door (John 10:9), the Good Shepherd (John 10:11), the Way, the Truth, and the Life (John 14:6), and the source for good works as the Vine (John 15:5). In the rest of the New Testament, Jesus is described as the head of the church (Eph. 1:22–23; 4:14–16; Rom. 12:4–5), the cornerstone of the church (Matt. 21:42; Acts 4:11–12; Eph. 2:20–22), and the bridegroom of the church (2 Cor. 11:2; Eph. 5:25–33; Rev. 19:7–9; 21:2, 9–11). What metaphor of Jesus has helped your faith?

April 27: Death of Jesus

Jesus' Death is the act that vicariously accomplished the final death and atoning of sin for believers. In the Catholic church, there is a focus put on the *Christ's Passion,* which is *not only the death of Jesus, but also the events leading up to it* (betrayal, arrest, trials, and torture). Although these instances show humility and pain in fulfilling prophecies, it is Christ's death on the cross that affects sin and death (Rom. 5:12, 15). Although God instituted a sacrificial system in the OT, those sacrifices could not actually do anything (Isa. 1:11; Heb. 10:4), but they were pointing to Jesus' death, which could (Heb. 10:11–14). Only Jesus' death is expiatory (take sins away) and propitiatory (appeases God's wrath). It is this substitution of Jesus for believers that accomplishes salvation. How can we worship Jesus with a better understanding of His death?

April 28: Burial of Jesus

The Burial of Jesus is the event that demonstrates both Jesus' death and resurrection were genuine. Jesus gave the prediction of the "sign of Jonah" in His ministry, saying He would be dead for three days and rise (Matt. 12:40). Some Christian sects believe that the Apostle's Creed and some Scriptures seem to allude to the *Harrowing of Hell*, or *the belief that Jesus rescued OT saints from Hades to bring them with Him to Heaven* (Eph. 4:9–10; 1 Pet. 3:18–20). Jesus' burial demonstrates that He did not just swoon or faint, that His body was not stolen or substituted, and that He did not have a twin that took His place. How does His entrance into the tomb, it's sealing, and it's being empty fill you with hope?

April 29: Resurrection of Jesus

The Resurrection is the act of Jesus' return to life from the dead which is the foundation of Christianity and the source of the Church's resurrection in the End. Paul told the Corinthians that the Christian faith was in vain if Jesus had not rose from the dead (1 Cor. 15:14). Jesus showed His wounds to his followers (Luke 24:39; John 20:20), ate with His disciples (Luke 24:36–43; John 21:1–14), and appeared to over 500 people (1 Cor. 15:3–7). The early rise of the church demonstrates Jesus' resurrection as the church endured through persecution, attested by authors such as Tacitus, Seutonius, and Josephus. Jesus' resurrection is the first fruits of all resurrections (1 Cor. 15:20), and ensures the believer's eternal life. The world has been positively affected by this truth being brought to all nations. How can we better worship the resurrected Jesus?

April 30: Ascension of Jesus

The Ascension of Jesus is the act of His return to heaven in his glorified body after His resurrection. Jesus told the disciples that He was going to go and prepare a place for them in heaven (John 14:2–3). In Acts, Jesus is watched in His ascension, and it is also explained that He will return the same way (Acts 1:9–11). It is from this heavenly position where Jesus is seated next to God the Father (Heb. 1:3; 1 Pet. 3:22) interceding on our behalf (Rom. 8:34). Because of the believer's connection to the Holy Spirit and through the Trinity's mutual indwelling, as Jesus is presently seated at the Father's right hand, the Christian is considered that way, too (Eph. 2:6), even when we are actually still presently living our lives on Fallen earth. How does our sure hope of resurrection because of Jesus' resurrection and ascension fuel your worship?

May: God the Holy Spirit

May 1: Pneumatology

An often-overlooked area of theology concerns one of the most necessary persons: The Holy Spirit. *Pneumatology is the study of God the Holy Spirit and His ministry in the lives of humanity, especially those who make up the Church.* In the New Testament, the Holy Spirit is clearly spoken of as an individual person who is God (Gen. 1:1–2; Acts 5:3–4), is separate from the Father and the Son (Matt. 28:19; Mark 1:9–11), and has unique ministries that only God can perform (1 Cor. 12:11; 2 Pet. 1:21). But, in the Old Testament, the Holy Spirit is only occasionally referenced, and His ministries are not as numerous as they are in the NT. This does not mean that the Holy Spirit is absent in the OT, only His ministry is highlighted in the NT. How can we determine what the Holy Spirit does and who He is?

May 2: Binitarianism

Because the OT is not entirely clear on who the Holy Spirit is, and because the NT puts most of its emphasis on God the Father and God the Son, some hold to a view called "binitarianism." *Binitarianism is the belief that there are only two persons that make up the Godhead, the Father and the Son.* Some have argued that, against the traditional view that the Jews were monotheists, ancient Israelites believed in two Gods in heaven. Typically, the god-like Angel of the Lord mentioned with God is seen as an example of God seen as only two persons. But, from the Trinitarian vantage-point of the NT, it is clear that the "Spirit" (Gen. 1:1–2; Num. 27:18; Judg. 6:34; 13:25), the Father, and the Son ("Lord," Ps. 110:1), all appear separately as God. How can we better worship the Holy Spirit as part of the Trinity?

May 3: Fellowship

Fellowship is the doctrine that speaks of the relationship amongst the Godhead in the Trinity and, through the Holy Spirit, amongst the Church. The Greek term translated "fellowship" is *koinonia*. In what manner is that fellowship amongst the Godhead has been a question of speculation. *Perichoresis* in Greek and *Circumincession* in Latin are two terms that are used for *the mutual indwelling of the Godhead.* It is through this mutual indwelling that Christ can indwell us through the Holy Spirit (Rom. 8:9–10). The *koinonia* of the Trinity is the precursor to and ultimate source of relationships experienced by created beings, especially humanity that is created in God's image. But it is also the basis for the fellowship Christians have through the indwelling of the Holy Spirit. How can your relationships reflect God's fellowship?

May 4: Subordinationism

Subordinationism is the view that there is an understood hierarchy within the Godhead. Although ranking the members of the Trinity seems problematic in any way, there can be a more heretical and acceptable way depending on how subordination is understood. If either the Son or the Holy Spirit are said to be lesser in being than God the Father, then that subordinationism was deemed heretical at the Council of Constantinople in AD 381. This is because no member of the Trinity can be greater or lesser in being than each other. But if one is arguing that the Son or the Spirit is subject to operating in a subordinate role to the Father, then this is less of a problem, although debatable. How can we determine if the Spirit has a subordinate role?

May 5: Procession

The Procession of the Spirit is the doctrine that speaks of who sent the Holy Spirit to minister to the Church. The entire Church agrees that the Holy Spirit proceeds from the Father (John 14:16, 26). The controversy of this doctrine begins with the addition of what is called the *filioque* ("and the Son") clause that appeared in the Constantinopolitan Creed sometime after AD 381. This phrase argued that the Holy Spirit proceeds from both the Father and the Son (John 15:26; 16:7), which ultimately helped lead to the Great Schism of the Roman Catholic and Eastern Orthodox churches in 1054, with the West accepting *filioque*, and the East rejecting it. To further confusion, there is debate as to whether this procession is eternal or not, as the Spirit could have been temporarily sent by the Son for Pentecost. Do you agree with the *filioque* clause?

May 6: Pentecost

The Pentecost after Jesus' ascension is the event where the Holy Spirit was given to the Church for salvation and ministry. After His resurrection, Jesus told His disciples to wait in Jerusalem until they receive power from on high (Luke 24:49; Acts 1:4). The Feast of Weeks, or *Shavuot* in the OT, and Pentecost in the NT take place 50 days after Passover. *Shavout* is one of the Pilgrim Feasts, so Jewish people from all around the Roman Empire would have traveled to Jerusalem to celebrate. Because of this, when the Holy Spirit comes in Acts 2, the gift of tongues is seen as a sign along with a blowing of wind and tongues of fire over peoples' heads. How does it help your faith to know when the Holy Spirit began permanently indwelling believers?

May 7: Breath

Breath is a term associated with the Holy Spirit and is translated from the same word as "spirit" in Hebrew and Greek. Both *ruach* in Hebrew and *pneuma* in Greek can be translated as "breath." The connection of breath and spirit in the ancient world may be because only the living had breath, and both breath and spirit were moving and invisible. The Holy Spirit is linked with breath in the NT a few times. First, Jesus breathes on the disciples after appearing to them, telling them to receive the Holy Spirit (John 20:22). The Word of God is also said to be God-breathed (*theopneustos*, 2 Tim. 3:16–17), which could relate the Spirit's role in the creation of Scripture. The association of the term "breath" with life could also be in the Spirit's role of giving the believer new life from Jesus' resurrection. How can you worship the Holy Spirit as the "Breath of God"?

May 8: Wind

The Holy Spirit is not only associated with breath, but also with wind. *Wind is a term associated with the Holy Spirit and is translated from the same word as "spirit" in Hebrew and Greek.* Both *ruach* in Hebrew and *pneuma* in Greek can be translated as "wind." Both terms may translate to breath, wind, and spirit because of their invisibility and movement. There are a few times where the Holy Spirit is tied to the concept of wind in the New Testament. When He speaks with Nicodemus, Jesus states that "the wind bloweth where it listeth" when referring to the Holy Spirit's ministry (John 3:8). At the Pentecost event in Acts 2, a sound like rushing wind came from Heaven when the Holy Spirit was given. How can you worship the Holy Spirit as the powerful force that He is?

May 9: Dove

The Dove is a bird that is associated with the Holy Spirit in the Scriptures. The dove appears in a lot of texts in the Bible, but it is not seen as the Holy Spirit every time. In fact, the only time it is used to represent the Holy Spirit specifically is at the Baptism of Jesus (Matt. 3:16; Mark 1:10; Luke 3:22; John 1:32). Even here, the language used is "like a dove," with Luke adding "bodily," indicating that the Holy Spirit was not a dove, but His descent seemed visually like one. Interestingly, the dove is a bird that is more associated with God than others. The flood account in Genesis shows a dove finding land where a raven failed (Gen. 8:6–12). Doves are also seen as innocent, being the option for the poor for sacrifices in the Law (Lev. 1:14; 5:7; Luke 2:24; Matt. 10:16). How can we better worship the innocent Holy Spirit?

May 10: Fire

Fire can be seen in some of the theophanies in Scripture, and is often used as a type for God's power. We can see fire used as theophanies in the Abrahamic Covenant (Gen. 15:17), the burning bush (Exod. 3:1–14), and the pillar of fire and smoke (Exod. 13:21–22; 14:19–29). At Pentecost, one of the signs of the Holy Spirit's coming to humanity was visible tongues of fire over the people there (Acts 2:3). In the Old and New Testaments, God's judgment of humanity is likened to a refining fire, purifying metal or burning up waste (Mal. 3:2; 1 Cor. 3:13). Finally, fire is used regarding the final judgment, where everyone separated from God ends up being thrown into the lake of fire for all eternity (Rev. 20:10–15). How can we have awe for God in His likeness to fire?

May 11: Anointing

Anointing is an act of the Holy Spirit that is given to Jesus for His messiahship and to believers for our new status in Christ. Anointing as the practice of rubbing or pouring oil on someone else to recognize a new status has been practiced throughout the Old Testament. For Jesus' status as the Messiah, or the "Anointed One," He would need more than just recognition from humanity. So, the Holy Spirit as a Godly authority anointed Jesus for His messiahship (Luke 4:18). But the Holy Spirit also anoints believers, as well. When we believe the Gospel, the Holy Spirit's anointing gains us other ministries of the Holy Spirit (2 Cor. 1:21), specifically including His ministry of teaching us the truths taught in Scripture (1 John 2:20, 27). How can we as those anointed by God Himself use our blessings to better know and serve God and others?

May 12: Earnest

An earnest payment in economics is an initial payment to show good faith to a seller that you will pay more later for an expensive purchase. In theology, *the Earnest is our receiving the Holy Spirit that God gives us to demonstrate He will give us eternal life with Him in heaven.* Today, we often use this term in buying property, but this concept has been around for a long time due to human fraudulence. In 2 Corinthians 1:22, Paul speaks of the Holy Spirit's ministry of sealing as well as the concept of His being an earnest in our heart. This language is repeated in 2 Corinthians 5:5 and Ephesians 1:14 as encouragement for us to have confidence in God's promise of eternal life because of this earnest payment. How does the Spirit's earnest give you hope?

May 13: Comforter

The Comforter is the title and ministry of the Holy Spirit that sees Him being with and aiding believers in Jesus' bodily absence. During Jesus' time with His disciples in the upper room, He begins to speak of a Comforter that will be sent by God to be with them when Jesus leaves them (John 14:16). The term used in this passage is *parakletos*, which suggests one who comes alongside someone, like an advocate, comforter, consoler, or counselor. This Paraclete is the Holy Spirit, who Jesus said would teach and help believers remember His teaching in His absence (John 14:26), as well as testify of Jesus (John 15:26). The Spirit's coming to be with us is also more intimate than Jesus' presence because the Spirit can indwell believers where Jesus has a bodily nature (John 16:7). How can we worship the Comforter?

May 14: Intercession

Intercession is the doctrine where one of the members of the Godhead speaks or prays on behalf of human beings. Both the Holy Spirit and Jesus are said to intercede for individual people. Jesus is said to intercede on our behalf to the Father in His current position at the Father's right hand (Rom. 8:34; Heb. 7:25). This could be because of His identification with us as human beings and because of the Father's transcendence (Heb. 4:15). But the Holy Spirit also acts as one who can pray for us. The distinction is that we are told by Paul that the Spirit prays for us when we are not even sure what to say (Rom. 8:26–27). How can we as believers better worship these Persons of the Godhead as we are now able to approach the Holy God as fallen, yet redeemed, people who pray with imperfect words?

May 15: Illumination

Illumination is the doctrine that speaks of the Holy Spirit's ability to make believers better understand and remember God's Word. In the upper room, before His death, burial, and resurrection, Jesus tells the disciples that He will send a Comforter that will teach the disciples and bring to remembrance all the things Jesus taught them (John 14:26). Paul tells the Corinthian church that believers have the mind of Christ because of the Spirit, and that it is the Holy Spirit that teaches us spiritual reality (1 Cor. 2:6–16). Peter also speaks of the Holy Spirit's hand in bringing about God's Word through the Old Testament prophets and the apostles in the New Testament, as well as the realization of scriptural truth by the believers who are indwelt by the Holy Spirit (1 Pet. 1:10–12). How can we better worship the Holy Spirit who illuminates?

May 16: Conviction

Conviction is the ministry of the Holy Spirit that brings to mind the weight of sin to a human. All people experience some sort of guilt or shame from sinful actions (Rom. 1:18; 2:15), but there is a difference between a human's having a conscience and their being convicted by the Holy Spirit. Jesus tells us that, when the Holy Spirit comes, He will convict the world of sin (John 16:8). It seems that, in addition to a human conscience, the Holy Spirit can draw attention to sin in anyone's lives. This could be a part of being called by the Spirit. But, as the Holy Spirit exclusively indwells believers, there is also an understanding that this conviction can be a more regular occurrence in the life of the Christian. How can we better worship the Holy Spirit in His convicting?

May 17: Indwelling

Indwelling is the doctrine that speaks of the Holy Spirit permanently residing in a believer. Where we see examples of spiritual beings possessing physical beings in the Scriptures (Mark 5:1–20), these beings are able to be exorcised from people and the possessed are subject to being controlled by the possessors. The Holy Spirit, on the other hand, indwells someone upon their belief (1 John 4:15) and that indwelling lasts for the duration of that person's life (John 14:16) as the believer is now one of many temples that the Holy Spirit resides in instead of the Tabernacle or Temple building (1 Cor. 3:16–17; 6:19; 2 Cor. 6:16). Indwelling is not the same as filling or control by the Holy Spirit, as people can still sin while having the Holy Spirit indwelling (Eph. 4:30). How can the Spirit's indwelling enable us to live out Christ's life (Gal. 2:20)?

May 18: Baptism of the Holy Spirit

The Baptism of the Holy Spirit is the ministry of the Holy Spirit that places us in the body of Christ. John's baptism signified the Holy Spirit baptism that began at Pentecost (Matt. 3:11; Mark 1:8; Luke 3:16; John 1:33; Acts 1:5). Any human can be baptized into the body of Christ (1 Co. 12:13), but the Holy Spirit's baptism is exclusively provided to those who believe (Acts 11:17). There is not another baptism that accomplishes this action (Eph. 4:5). The baptism of the Holy Spirit that we receive upon belief is different than our water baptism, and it is also different than the indwelling or the filling of the Holy Spirit that are all referenced in the New Testament. If those who believe are baptized in the Holy Spirit and unified in Christ, how can we better worship the Spirit who baptizes us?

May 19: Filling

The Filling of the Spirit is the doctrine where the Holy Spirit empowers the believer. Where the baptism of the Holy Spirit and His indwelling are permanent acts, the filling of the Spirit seems to be something that can happen to a believer at different times (Acts 2:4; 4:31). The concept of filling also seems to have the understanding of affecting or influencing someone like alcohol can, or, at least, the two are contrasted with each other (Eph. 5:18). To what degree this influence can have on believers is unknown, but many people in the Scriptures have been filled with the Holy Spirit (Exod. 28:3; Judg. 14:6; Acts 4:8–9; 7:55–56). We are also exhorted in Ephesians 5:18 to be filled with the Spirit, reiterating its limited and repeating nature. If the Holy Spirit can fill those who have already been baptized in the Holy Spirit, how can we be filled and serve in this filling?

May 20: Sealing

The Sealing of the Spirit is the doctrine that speaks of the believer's being kept by God until glory. The act of sealing happens the moment that someone believes (2 Cor. 1:22; Eph. 4:30), and it lasts until we are with Jesus in the End (Eph. 1:13). The concept of sealing in the ancient world is when an authority would send an important message on paper or clay with his mark on it. That seal would mean that only the intended receiver of the message could read the message, and, with the medium of paper, a wax seal would have to be broken to show it has been received and read. For the believer, the Holy Spirit acts as a seal of God's authority over Christians until our appointed time. How can we better worship the Holy Spirit who seals us?

May 21: Fruit of the Spirit

The Fruit of the Spirit is the result that comes from the Holy Spirit's ministry through the believer. Although there are probably an innumerable number of results that can come of the Holy Spirit's work in us, the main list comes from Galatians 5:22–23. The list of spiritual fruit produced by the Holy Spirit includes: love (*agape*), joy (*chara*), peace (*eirene*), patience/longsuffering (*makrothymia*), kindness (*chrestotes*), goodness (*agathosyne*), faith[fullness] (*pistis*), gentleness (*prautes*), and self-control (*enkrateia*). Paul also adds that there is no law against these things, suggesting we can produce as much of this fruit as possible and it will never be sinful. Although the fruit that Jesus mentioned in John 15:1–17 seems to be bringing about other believers, could this abiding connection be how Spiritual fruit is produced as well?

May 22: Spiritual Gifts

Spiritual Gifts are special abilities that the Holy Spirit provides believers to help others in the body of Christ. There are several lists that mention the Spiritual Gifts (1 Cor. 12:8–10, 29–30; Rom. 12:6–8; Eph. 4:11), this is a compiled list of all mentioned: wisdom (*sophia*), knowledge (*gnosis*), faith (*pistis*), healing (*iama*), miracles (*dunamis*), prophecy (*propheteia*), discernment (*diakrisis*), tongues (*glossa*) and interpretation of tongues (*ermeneia*), apostleship (*apostolos*), teaching (*didaskalia*), helping/ministry (*diakonia*), administration (*kyberneseis*), encouragement (*paraklesis*), giving (*metadidomi*), leadership (*proistemi*), mercy (*eleeo*), evangelism (*evangelistes*), and pastor (*piomens*). Although these lists may not be exhaustive, what spiritual gift do you think you have and how can you use it to benefit the Church?

May 23: Sign Gifts

Sign Gifts are a series of gifts that were used as signs and that may or may not still be in use. Three sign gifts, tongues, knowledge, and prophecy, are in contention in Paul's first letter to the Corinthians. Paul tells us those three will one day cease when the "perfect" comes (1 Cor. 13:10) where love will not (1 Cor. 13:8). If the "perfect" is Scripture, these gifts are not needed now. If it is Jesus, they are here until the End. The debate over tongues today is whether they are a missionary language (Acts 2), a prayer language (Rom. 8:26–27), or an angelic language (1 Cor. 13:1). *Continuationists believe sign gifts are for today*, and *Cessationists believe sign gifts are not for today*. How might these passages and the rest of Scripture help us take a position?

May 24: Miracles

Miracles are works performed by God, often through an intermediary, to show God's power over creation. Because God created everything, people can see everything as miraculous. But miracles are not natural, so they are not repeatable or reoccurring events. This means that the Christian should have more of a narrow understanding of miracles than having a broad view of them. This limits the scope of what we call a miracle to God's intentional manipulation of the natural order of things to show His power over creation. Some general examples of miracles include God giving children to Sarah and leading the Israelites across the Red Sea, with specific events mentioned as miracles being Moses staff turning into a snake (Exod. 7:9), the feeding of the 5,000 (John 6:14), and healing (Acts 4:22). How do miracles strengthen your faith?

May 25: Signs and Wonders

Signs and Wonders are miraculous works in Scripture that are usually performed to demonstrate God's authority. Signs and wonders are often mentioned together and often for demonstration purposes (Dan. 4:2–3; 6:27). These are great displays of power. Unfortunately, signs and wonders are not always positive. The plagues God performs through Moses onto Egypt are often referred to as signs and wonders (Exod. 7:3, Deut. 34:11). In the New Testament, Jesus criticizes those always looking for signs and wonders (John 4:48), and He says false teachers will perform them (Matt. 24:24; Mark 13:22). Although Jesus speaks a blessing over those who believe without signs (John 20:29), how can belief in signs and wonders of God strengthen your faith?

May 26: Praying in the Spirit

Praying in the Spirit is the ministry of the Holy Spirit that helps us pray when we do not know what to say. This doctrine specifically comes from Romans 8:26–27, and the concept seems to be that when we are not sure what to say, the Holy Spirit prays on our behalf. This can also be a part of the intercessory work of the Holy Spirit. For some, the "groaning" in this passage has to do with the gift of tongues, as it is argued that the Holy Spirit actually speaks through people in an unintelligible language. But in this passage, the Holy Spirit's groaning "cannot be uttered," and, therefore, this does not seem to be a passage linked to tongues, which is seemingly audible (Acts 2). How can the Holy Spirit's prayer for us when we are at a loss of words bring us comfort, and how can we know when these prayers are done on our behalf?

May 27: Lying to the Spirit

Lying to the Spirit seems to be an act that can result in the liar's death. The only account we have of something like this happening is in Acts 5:1–11. In the preceding chapter (Acts 4:32–37), we see that the early church decided to share all of their possessions so that no one lacked anything. But a couple named Ananias and Sapphira withheld some or all of their wealth. Peter told Ananias that he was filled with Satan and lied to God, and both Ananias and Sapphira died three hours apart from each other. The witnesses were said to be afraid after seeing this. Other signs and wonders follow this event, making this a holy demonstration. There are other negative ways humans can act towards the Spirit, but do you believe that this is a repeatable action by the Spirit or a single event?

May 28: Grieving the Spirit

Grieving the Spirit seems to be a sinful action that people can do that demonstrates the Holy Spirit's personhood through emotion. The passage that speaks of this action is in Ephesians 4:30–32. Here, in a list of exhortations to the Ephesian church to not commit certain sins that are now inconsistent with our new lives in Christ, Paul mentions that the members of the church should not "grieve" the Holy Spirit. An interesting aspect to this is the fact that it is implied that only Christians can commit this sin. That does not necessarily mean that unbelievers cannot do this action, but it might indicate that this action is performed by people otherwise loyal and connected to the Holy Spirit, causing pain to someone in a close relationship. How can we as believers make sure that we do not grieve the Holy Spirit in our relationship with Him?

May 29: Quenching the Spirit

Quenching the Spirit seems to be a sinful action that people can do that limits the work of the Holy Spirit. In 1 Thessalonians 5:19, in a list of exhortations to the Thessalonian church to not commit certain sins now inconsistent with our new lives in Christ, Paul mentions that the members of the church should not "quench" the Holy Spirit. Although we cannot know what this means definitely, the word translated "quench" (*sbennumi*) is used in other passages for extinguishing flames (Matt. 25:8; Mark 9:44, 46). This may mean that believers are in some way able to impede the work of the Holy Spirit, either in their own lives or in others. If this is true and is possible for the believer, how can we make sure that we do not impede the work of the Holy Spirit?

May 30: Blasphemy of the Spirit

Blasphemy of the Spirit is the one unforgiveable sin that a person can commit. The texts that speak about this issue are Matthew 12:31–32 and Mark 3:28–29. Before these passages, the scribes and Pharisees claimed that Jesus Himself was not casting out demons, but Beelzebub was doing so through Him. Jesus, stating how that would be impossible, explained that a house divided against itself cannot stand. He then explains that all sins, including blasphemy, can be forgiven by God except for blasphemy of the Holy Spirit, which would make one in danger of eternal damnation. It is not entirely sure what blasphemy against the Holy Spirit would be, but many have suggested that it is simply unbelief in the gospel or the work of the Holy Spirit. If blasphemy against the Holy Spirit is the only unpardonable sin, how can we make sure this does not happen?

May 31: Testing the Spirits

Testing the Spirits seems to be an action that people can do to determine whether something is of God or not. The verse in question is from 1 John 4:1–3. Here, after John distinguishes between what marks those in Christ and what marks those not in Christ, he exhorts believers not to believe all spirits. Spirits of God will confess Jesus came in flesh and is God, and Spirits not of God will not confess this. Where this comes to harm the church is through the work of false teachers and prophets. After discerning the spirit or Spirit behind a teaching, the Christian engages in spiritual warfare (2 Cor. 10:3–5), of which Paul says there is armor (Eph. 6:10–17) and a sword (Eph. 6:17; Heb. 4:12), and that we are to pray and keep a watch out for others (Eph. 6:18). How do you test the spirits and engage in spiritual warfare?

June: Angels

June 1: Angelology

In addition to understanding God, God's Word, and human beings, another important area of study in Systematic Theology is that of angelic beings. *Angelology is the study of the nature, ranks, and actions of spiritual creatures.* Angelology is a complex discipline because various terms are used throughout Scripture to refer to limited positive and negative spirit beings. These terms are also sometimes used for beings and things that are not angelic, and there are also terms that refer to both good and bad spiritual beings. To add to the confusion, there is information about spiritual creatures in the Bible, but there is also extra-biblical information about these beings that is non-canonical, yet often used by authors of Scripture. How can you study angels well?

June 2: Angels

Generally, *Angels are limited beings created by God that are spiritual in nature, but specifically they are spiritual beings with the task of being messengers of God.* The terms we translate and transliterate into "angel" are *malak* in the Hebrew, and *angelos* in the Greek, both meaning "messenger." Angels are limited creatures and do not have divine attributes. The origin of angels is unclear, but it is often suggested that, because angels can also be called "stars," passages that refer to heavens being created are also when angelic beings are created (Gen. 2:1; Neh. 9:6; Ps. 33:6). Angels are often seen as bodily figures and often provoke awe (Gen. 19; Acts 10:1–8). For the broad category of angelic beings, there are many individual and groups of angels with different ranks and ministries. How can our understanding of angels better show God's greatness?

June 3: Incorporeality

The Incorporeality of angels is the concept that angelic beings are not bodily in nature, but are spiritual beings that are limited in presence and time. Angels are creatures that are not eternal, as they were created by God at a certain point. Unlike humanity, they do not experience physical death. This spirituality that is limited in both presence and time extends to fallen angels. This is how one demon can possess individuals but not groups, yet multiple demons can possess an individual (Mark 5:1–10; Luke 8:26–39). There are issues with the incorporeality of angels, in that they can be seen (Isa. 6:1–3) and offered food (Gen. 18:1–8) in addition to other ways they interact with the physical world. How does incorporeality help us view angels, God, and man?

June 4: Innumerable

Because angels were created in one event, a question one might have is, "how many angelic beings were created in this event?" The answer the Bible provides is "innumerable" (Heb. 12:22). *Innumerable means that there is so much of something that it would be difficult to quantify just how much of it there is.* Examples often used for things that are innumerable in Scripture are sand and stars (Gen. 22:17). This concept coupled with the idea of angelic incorporeality led to some mocking theological speculation by suggesting early theologians would argue over how many angels could dance on the head of a pin. If Rev.12:4 has the total amount of demons that fight alongside Satan in the End, this would seem to indicate a third of the innumerable angels are fallen. How can our knowledge of the number of angels help us see God's greatness?

June 5: Divine Council

The Divine Council is the corpus of spiritual beings that work together with or for God on His behalf. The term *Elohim generally means gods, with "El" being the singular for God.* But also, *Elohim can be used for great beings in Scripture, whether God, people, or angelic beings.* The angelic elohim make up the divine council (*sod*), sometimes called an assembly (*edah/mo'ed*), congregation (*qahal*), court (*din*), heavenly or holy ones, or host (*saba*). They typically worship and stand in agreement with God, deliver His messages, and partner with Him. The beings that make up the council are not perfect (Job 15:15), and are able to fall away from God. How can the Divine Council help us better understand God and His work? *Ref: Deut. 32:8–9; Ps. 82; 1 Kgs. 22:19–23; Dan. 7:9–10*

June 6: Sons of God

Sons of God are beings that are under the Father's authority, either as groups of people or spiritual beings. Angelic beings are often referred to as "sons of God" or "sons of the Most High" in Scripture. Much like the Israelites in the Old Testament or Christians in the New Testament, angelic beings share a close relationship to God, being on His team, or divine council. An area where this shared terminology affects theology is in the lead up to the flood account in Genesis 6. Here, if the "sons of God" are godly people who mix with the "daughters of men," then it seems that the flood can be, at least in part, due to the faithful joining with the unfaithful people. If the "sons of God" are angelic, there is a potential that spiritual beings mixing with humanity could be the cause. How can we be encouraged by sharing this title with angels?

June 7: Hierarchy of Angels

The Hierarchy of Angels speaks of the rank of angelic beings in their relation to God or other angels. In addition to the terms referring to the jobs, groups, and nature of angels, there are terms that refer to the position of angels. Some terms in the NT referring to angelic positions are thrones (*thronos*), rulers/principalities (*arche*), powers (*exousia*), might (*dunamis*), dominions (*kuriotes*), and dignities (*doxa*). Along with Old Testament terms like cherubim and seraphim, as well as there being archangels compared to regular angels, many have sought to compile these terms of the hierarchy of angels in structured lists and charts. How does our understanding or angelic rank help us better know our ordered God? *Ref: Col. 1:16; 2:15; Eph. 1:21; 3:10; Jude 1:8.*

June 8: Archangels

Archangels seem to be higher level, and often named, angels with additional ministries other than being only messengers of God. As with much of the study of angelic beings, there is biblical data that we can look at, but there is extra-biblical data, as well, that can make our understanding of archangels more challenging. In the Bible, there are two recorded archangels: Michael and Gabriel. In the extra-biblical book of Enoch, Raphael, Remiel, Reuel, Sariel, and Uriel are added. Gabriel appeared to Daniel (Dan. 8:15–26; 9:21–27), Zechariah (Luke 1:11–20), and Mary (Luke 1:26–38). Michael is called the chief prince (Dan. 10:13, 21) and is seen as one who is often in battle (Dan. 12:1; Rev. 12:7), with Jude even referencing an unknown, extra-biblical text about Michael arguing with Satan (Jude 1:9). How can archangels help us understand angels?

June 9: Seraphim

Seraphim are angelic creatures that have three sets of wings, dwell in the throne room of God, and are associated with fiery serpents. Saraph can mean burning or serpents, which come together in the story about the fiery serpents (called *nachash*) in Numbers 21. It is also used for what Isaiah finds in the throne room of God (Isa. 6). Isaiah sees creatures with one set of wings covering their face, one set covering their feet, and one set helping to fly. These beings are associated with holiness, as they praise God, singing "holy, holy, holy," and they cleanse Isaiah's unclean lips with a burning coal. In Revelation 4, the four beasts in the throne room also sing "holy, holy, holy" and have six wings but are covered in eyes and have the eagle, lion, man, and ox motif. How can the seraph's worship encourage ours?

June 10: Cherubim

Cherubim are angelic creatures that have two wings, with features like eagles, lions, men, and oxen, whose images are used in the decoration of the temple. Cherubim are first mentioned in the Bible is as guardians of the Garden of Eden after Adam and Eve were expelled (Gen. 3:24). When Ezekiel compares the prince of Tyre to Satan and his fall, he refers to him as an "anointed cherub" (Ezek. 28:11–19), pushing that term back to before the Fall. Cherubim have two wings (Exod. 25:20; 37:9) and appear with the faces of an eagle, lion, man, and ox (Ezek. 1:10), similar to the "living creatures" in Revelation 4. Cherubim are carved on the lid of the ark and appear on the curtain in the temple (Exod. 36:35; 37:7–9). How do these guards show God's holiness?

June 11: Satanology

Satanology is the study of the nature, names, and works of the Adversary, or "Satan." In studying Satan, the Christian's goal is merely to understand him in a "know your enemy" sense, and not to have "sympathy for the devil." Because of human interest, famous authors like Dante, Milton, and Goethe have written extra-biblical texts about Satan in order to fill the gaps of understanding that God has intentionally left blank in the Scriptures. But the correct course for mankind in this study is to rely on the authoritative, inspired Word of God to provide us with the information that we need to know about our adversary. The Bible does describe Satan through his names and works, allusions to his fall, and clarity regarding his ultimate end. How can we have comfort in the Bible's explanation of our enemy?

June 12: Satan

Satan is the name of the ultimate adversary of God and God's people in the Bible. Satan, or "adversary," can be used of people other than the figure Satan in the Bible, even for the angel of the Lord (Num. 22:22, 32; 1 Chr. 21:1; 2 Sam. 24:1–2). "*The Satan*" (Job 1, 2; Zech. 3) could be a positive adversary working for God, if he is not "Satan." The limited creature of God that is seen as a tempting serpent in the garden (Gen. 3; 2 Cor. 11:3) seems to be an anointed cherub that was cast out of heaven (Isa. 14:3–23, Ezek. 28:2–19, Luke 10:17–20; Rev. 12:7–9). His work is as a liar (John 8:44) and tempter (Matt. 4:3), and his ultimate end is to the lake of fire (Rev. 20:10). He is known as Beelzebul (Mark 3:22), a dragon (Rev. 12:3), and evil one (1 John 2:13). How can knowing Satan's limitations and end bring us comfort?

June 13: The Serpent

The Serpent is the figure in the Garden of Eden that leads the first man and woman to disobey God. The term for "serpent" in Genesis 3 is *nachash*, which is a word for snake. But the serpent in this passage has anthropomorphic speech that it uses to question God in its conversation with Eve. There is a link between snakes and angelic figures in the OT with the term *saraph* being used for both snakes and an angelic creature. But since this serpent, as well as a dragon, is linked to Satan in the New Testament (Rev. 12:9; 20:2), it is most likely that these would be forms that the cherub Satan takes. The serpent is cursed by God, with the protoevangelium telling of the seed of the woman (Jesus) bruising the serpent's (Satan's) head (destruction) when the serpent only bruises Jesus' heel (crucifixion). What does Satan's being a serpent mean for him?

June 14: The Tempter

The Tempter is a name for Satan that refers to his first action towards humanity. In Genesis 3, Satan comes to Adam and Eve in the likeness of a serpent. Here, by questioning God and lying, he tempts the first humans to disobey God. In the New Testament, this word is only used of Satan twice. The first is found in Matthew 4:3, and, instead of it speaking about the temptation of Adam and Eve in the Garden, it refers to Jesus' temptation by Satan in the wilderness before Jesus' ministry. The second time it is used is for Paul's desire for the Thessalonian church to not fall for false teaching in his absence. In these passages, we see that Satan's work of temptation appears to be continual until his end. How can we rely on God to avoid temptation?

June 15: The Devil

The Devil is the name of Satan that refers to his work as an accuser, slanderer, or liar. The Greek word that appears in the New Testament is *diabolos* and is used for an accuser or slanderer. In John 8:44, Jesus says that the devil is a liar and the father of lies. This is most likely referring to his lie in the garden (Gen. 3), but it can also appropriately apply to his self-deceit in Isaiah 14:14 and Ezekiel 28:17. His nature is deceitful, as well, as he is called *Lucifer* (*heylel*, "shining one"), and the "son of the morning." This is a reference to Venus, which is a lesser light can be seen during the day, and speaks of his brilliance, from which one would not anticipate evil. Spiritual warfare is, in large part, to withstand the lies of the devil, which God helps us with (Eph. 6:11), and can be from false teachers. How can you resist the devil's lies (Jas. 4:7)?

June 16: The Evil One

The Evil One is a title for Satan that speaks of his character and work. This word, *poneros*, is used for the overall character of Satan, as he is a hindrance to God's work (Matt. 13:19, 38; 1 John 3:12), as well as someone to overcome for the believer (1 John 2:13; 5:18). A similar term used for Satan, *Belial, is a term that becomes a name for Satan in between the testaments and speaks of his worthlessness. Belial* means "worthless," and is initially used in the Old Testament to speak of people of villainous character, which is ultimately worthless (Deut. 13:13; Judg. 19:22; 20:13; 1 Sam. 2:12). In the intertestamental period, it became a term for Satan, himself, with the apostle Paul even using this term for Satan (2 Cor. 6:15). How can we overcome Satan's efforts?

June 17: Beelzebul

Beelzebul and its variations are names for Satan that speak of his being the prince of the world. The name *Baal* means "lord," and it is also used as a title for God and of a Canaanite storm deity. Beelzebul is "the god of Ekron" (2 Kgs. 1) as well as a title used for the Baal in the Ugaritic "Baal Cycle" poetry. In the Scriptures, this title is associated with Satan as he is understood as the "prince of demons" (Matt. 12:24, 27; Mark 3:22; Luke 11:15). We also see Satan is called the "prince of the world" (John 12:31; 14:30; 16:11), the "god of this world" (2 Co. 4:4), and the "prince of the power of the air" (Eph. 2:2), speaking of the power that God has allowed him to have. A mocking name used in the NT is *Beelzebub*, or "lord of flies." As Satan has temporary ability from God to work his evil on the earth, how can we have comfort knowing his final end?

June 18: The Dragon

The Dragon is a title for Satan in the book of Revelation and speaks of his chaotic nature as well as linking back to the serpent. The term "dragon" in the OT is *tanniyn*, and, because of its association with sea monsters, it can be used for whales. Dragons in the OT and ANE cultures are associated with the sea and gods of the sea (*Yam* = sea, *Lotan* = Leviathan, and *Tiamat*) (Ps. 74:13–14). The ancient neighbors of Israel believed the sea was chaotic. They would write of their gods battling sea dragons and the sea, and the Israelites would write of God's authority and victory over the sea (Exod. 14; Josh. 3–4; Ps. 89:9–10). Satan is depicted as a dragon in Revelation (Rev. 12), and he and the sea are defeated in the end (Rev. 20:7–10; 21:1). How can we have peace in knowing chaos will cease?

June 19: The Destroyer

The Destroyer is the name of one or many angelic figures that God allows to cause destruction. This figure is often understood to be either Satan or a demonic or several demonic figures. The first time we see this figure, though, it is mentioned as the angel that was charged with killing the firstborn males at the Passover (Exod. 12:23). In the OT, many people are called "destroyer" (Job 15:21; Ps. 17:4; Prov. 28:24), even Samson (Judg. 16:24), but no demon is called this. Jeremiah likens Babylon to a destroyer of Gentiles and a lion (Jer. 4:7), and Peter describes Satan similarly (1 Pet. 5:8). Paul also references the destroyer as the one that killed some Israelites by fire in the Wilderness (Num. 11:1–3; 1 Cor. 10:10). In Revelation, *Apollyon* and *Abaddon* are names for the destroyer. How can God use this being to bring about His will?

June 20: Demonology

Demonology is the study of the nature, kinds, and work of demonic creatures. Demonology is a complicated field of study because of the limited and varied data that we have in the Bible. There are also many extra-biblical writings that the authors of Scripture are aware of that provide additional information about demons. In order to have the most accurate understanding of demons, it is appropriate for the Christian to first limit their study to the inspired, biblical information, and then examine any specific writings that the biblical authors allude to or reference. Then, logical deductions and later history can be examined. We should also be careful because demons are malevolent beings. Why would it be important for Christians to be aware of demonic creatures?

June 21: Demons

Demons are limited, yet powerful, spiritual creatures that are in rebellion towards God. It is not clear how demons began, but there are a few potentials. The first is that, whenever Satan rebelled and was cast out of heaven, a third of the angels fell with him (Rev. 12:4). But if this happened before Jesus' birth, why is it only mentioned in the book of Revelation? Another possibility is when the "sons of God" mix with the "daughters of men" in Genesis 6, but this requires mixing of physical and spiritual beings. Regardless of their origin, demons are intelligent creatures (Acts 16:16–18; Jas. 2:19) that perform negative actions, like possession, causing sickness (Matt. 9:32–33; Matt. 12:22; Mark 5:1–20; 7:26–30; Luke 4:33–36), and lying (Gal. 1:8; Eph. 6:12; 1 John 4:1–6). How can we live well with demons causing chaos to God's work?

June 22: Watchers

The Watchers are creatures in the extra-biblical text 1 Enoch that have ties to ancient Near Eastern literature. Biblical supremacy is important in formulating theology, including demonology. But some look at ANE literature and 1 Enoch as sources for the story of the *nephilim* in Genesis 6. The Watchers, mentioned in 1 Enoch, seem to correspond to seven pre-flood *apkallu* in texts like the Sumerian kings list, who gave knowledge to humanity. These *apkallu* mixed with humans to make four post-flood part human *apkallu* which would be the giant *nephilim*. First Enoch was written in between the OT and NT, it is referenced in the NT (Jude 1:6; 1 Pet. 3:14–22; 2 Pet. 2:4), and is influenced by OT and ANE texts. How can we best use non-canonical literature?

June 23: Rephaim

The Rephaim are giant, possibly demonic, beings that appear in the Old Testament as enemies of Israel. If ancient Near Eastern material is underlying Genesis 6:1–4, the *Rephaim* are human/god hybrid kings that have been sent to the underworld (*sheol*, *hades*, or *tartarus*). If this is the case, one theory is that these are the unclean (mixed) spirits in the NT that were killed by the Israelites in the conquest of Israel in Joshua. But, excluding extra-biblical texts, the *Rephaim* are seen to be a part of the giant clans in the OT, like the Anakim (Num. 13:32–33) and the Amonites and their kings (Sihon and Og of Bashan) (Deut. 2–3). These giants are seen as constant antagonists of Israel in the Old Testament, including the passages regarding Goliath and his brothers. How the judgment of the *Rephaim* give hope to Christians?

June 24: Azazel

Azazel is both the term for the scapegoat during the Day of Atonement and an extra-biblical demonic or Satanic figure. Originally, the *azazel* was the scapegoat let out into the wilderness for Israel's sin in the Day of Atonement (*Yom Kippur*) (Lev. 16). At some point, it gets associated with a demonic or Satanic being that appears in the book of 1 Enoch as a leader who brings secret knowledge from before the flood and is punished. In Leviticus 17, there seem to be "goat demons" (*saiyrim*) that the Israelites are commanded not to worship. The lore of Azazel and the "goat demons" seem to be creations that were made after the OT, but read about by the NT authors. In what way can Christians balance our understanding of what the OT authors wrote with the later interpretation that NT authors read?

June 25: Possession

Possession is the process by which a demonic figure takes control of a physical creature. There are many examples of possession in the Bible, but most are in the NT. In the OT, King Saul is tormented by an evil spirit (1 Sam. 16:14–15; 18:10–11; 19:9–10). Of the many examples of possession in the NT, most are associated with ailments (Matt. 9:32–34; 12:22; Luke 14:23). One time, Jesus casts out multiple demons named "Legion" (about 4,000–5,000 in a Roman legion) from a man and into a herd of pigs (Matt. 8:28–32; Mark 5:2–13; Luke 8:26–33). Here, we learn multiple demons can possess one person, and that demons can possess animals. It seems that even Satan can possess individuals (Luke 22:3). It does not appear that demons can possess believers, but they may oppress them with lies or attacks. How can we avoid demonic oppression?

June 26: Exorcism

Exorcism is the practice of extracting a demon from a possessed individual. In the New Testament, we have many examples of exorcisms, but exorcisms predate the New Testament. From the ancient Near East, there are cuneiform tablets that explain how to stop bad spirits from doing bad things by finding the spirit's name and then applying the right ritual to deter that bad spirit from causing harm. In the NT, we initially only see Jesus cast out demons, and the demons sometimes plead with Him beforehand (Mark 1:23; Luke 4:33). When the disciples and later apostles perform exorcisms, they do not find the demons' names, but they cast them out in Jesus' name (Mark 16:17; Acts 19:13). What does this switch in naming mean for Jesus' ultimate authority?

June 27: Magic

Magic is the manipulation or attempted manipulation of physical or spiritual reality by physical or spiritual means apart from God. In the Old Testament, Israel was commanded not to practice magic (Exod. 22:18; Lev. 19:31) with a long list of condemned practices in Deuteronomy 18:10–12, including: child sacrifice (*ma'abir beno ubitto ba'esh*), divination (*qesem*), omens (*me'nonen*), enchantment (*menahes*), sorcery (*mekassep*), charming (*chaber*), mediumship (*sha'el*), using familiars (*'ob*), conjuring (*weyidde'oni*), and necromancy (*doresh*). Throughout scripture, magic users are often seen as impotent (Exod. 7–8; 1 Sam. 28; Acts 8:9–25; 13:10–12). This does not mean that the attempt to manipulate nature or consort with demons is not, in itself, sinful. How can the enemies' lies in this area be understood as both serious yet impotent by us?

June 28: Idols

Idols are physical representations of gods. In the Bible, idolatry is seen as a grave sin. In the Ten Commandments, God explicitly commands the Israelites not to make or worship idols (Exod. 20:4–6; Deut. 5:8–10). This is because the other nations of the ANE used idolatry throughout much of the worship of their false gods. They would perform rituals to spiritually open the mouth of an idol so that a god could be present in the idol and eat offerings. Israel began to fall into idolatry in worshipping neighboring gods and even objects God used to help them (2 Ki. 18:4; Num. 21:4–9). They also worshipped idols in the temple (Ezek. 8). Idolatry is not just worshipping representations, but also things that replace God. How can we see and flee our current idols?

June 29: False Gods

False gods are figures throughout the world that compete for worship and the title of God in contrast to the one, true God of Israel. There are many gods referenced in Scripture, including Asherah (Exod. 34:13), Baal (2 Kgs. 18), Dagon (1 Sam. 5), Hermes (Acts 14:12), Marduk (Jer. 50:2), Molech (Lev. 20), Tammuz (Ezek. 8:14), and Zeus (Acts 14:12). There are many more gods referenced, and even insinuated gods, as the plagues of the Exodus could have demonstrated God's authority over Egypt's pantheon. There is even a reference to an unknown god in Athens just so one is not left out (Acts 17:23). The question is whether or not these gods are human fabrications or real demons stealing God's worship. Regardless of the facts of each instance, Yahweh alone is worthy of any worship. How can we determine between false gods and the one, true God?

June 30: Exotheology

Exotheology, or Astrotheology, is the study of alien life and their potential existence and works in relation to theology. There are many theories regarding aliens, alien life, their technology, and works from people outside of a Judeo-Christian worldview. *Panspermia is the concept that life was seeded onto Earth from extraterrestrial life. Ancient Astronaut Theory is the idea that alien life helped modernize the ancient world by building and providing technology.* But the concept of alien life in a Christian context provides problems. If there is sentient and/or sapient alien life outside of humanity, are they fallen? If not, what would that mean, and, if so, would they need a separate savior? The more likely potential is that alien sightings are demonic activity if they are not hallucinations. How should we view aliens?

July: Civics

July 1: Political Theology

Political Theology is the study of the intersection of Theology and politics generally, including political theories, civics, and sociology. Because both theological and political ideologies are philosophical, and because all people hold worldviews that affect their philosophy, our politics and theology are often influenced by how we understand reality or view the world. More narrowly, *Public Theology is how our theology intersects with our civic engagement.* Therefore, although there are many different political systems and positions that humans can hold, as a Christian, there will be a narrow selection of those views that aligns with our worldview, and even less given where we live, and we should seek what those are. How can we understand what our political options are and how we can live by them?

July 2: Order

Order is the concept of things being organized as they should be. In ancient contexts, the neighbors of Israel had stories about their gods fighting chaos to bring about order through conflict. In the biblical account of creation, God is orderly by nature and simply commands matter and time to be orderly. Because God is orderly, when He made mankind in His image, He gave us His desire for order, yet from our limited understanding and ability. This human desire for order continued through the Fall, and became even more distant from God's character. Therefore, God has spoken to man through His word in time to provide more insight to what correct order should be. In the OT, this concept is called *shalom*, and is often translated as "peace." How can we be more conformed to true order?

July 3: Ethics

Ethics is the study of morality and how one determines right and wrong or good and evil. In society, there are many problems that require an understanding and a taking of an active position on a particular ethical theory. Issues like determining whether or not certain people are born in a society (eugenics), how to treat those with disabilities, and whether or not we should assist people in dying (euthanasia) are all seen through our ethical lenses. For Christians, the basis for our ethical theories is God's Word. Therefore, when making ethical judgments in a society, we ought to consider what biblical principles underlie a particular issue and not changing factors like consensus. Virtue Ethics, Natural Law Theory, and Divine Command Theory are the typical ethical theories that Christians hold to. What ethical theory do you hold to?

July 4: Citizen

A Citizen is one individual that is part of a society. A citizen is a native or naturalized person who contributes positively to the state they live in. Part of the society's obligation for its people is to make decisions that allow for optimal conditions for as many citizens as possible. In exchange, citizens often have certain benefits, duties, and rights within a state that people outside of the same state do not have. In different societies, citizens may be able to own property, participate in the defense of their land or people in the land, and exchange goods and services with other citizens. Citizens engage in the culture of their community, and they may or may not have a say in the decisions of their state. What do the Scriptures say about being a good citizen in a society?

July 5: Family

A Family is a group of people connected by genetics, marriage, or adoption that continues on a genealogical lineage. Families are central to Scripture. All humanity shares a genealogical heritage that stems back to Adam and Eve. The people of Israel are a more specific family line that God began with Abraham, and they are the main focus of the Bible. Although a citizen is the basic unit of a civilization, the family units within a society are the primary foundation for a citizen's worldview, customs, and traditions. Families can connect with other families through marriages, and they can adopt people from outside their family lines. In the NT, Paul writes about family expectations, or household codes (*haustafeln*), where separate members of a family are provided with expectations (Eph. 5:22—6:9; Col. 3:18–4:1). What is a biblical family?

July 6: Singleness

Singleness is the state of an adult person outside of a marriage relationship. Although marriage seems to be the default relational mode for adult citizens, people can be without marriage for a period or they choose to live a life of singleness. In the NT, Paul seems to suggest that singleness is a gift for usefulness, and states that he wished all people could be single as he was (1 Cor. 7:7–9). Jesus was the ultimate example of singleness as he never married, but marriage seems to be the default position for pastors (1 Tim. 3:2). Because intercourse is relegated to the marriage relationship, it is important for the single person to practice celibacy. *Celibacy is the act of abstinence from intercourse.* How can we as citizens live out a life of singleness in light of God's desire for humanity to multiply?

July 7: Marriage

Marriage is the covenant of man and woman together as one unit. The covenant of marriage has been around since the creation of woman (Gen. 2:23–24). Biblically, marriages ought to be monogamous and between a man and woman. Although polygamy was practiced by persons in Scripture, these are descriptive explanations of events and not prescriptive. One of the primary reasons for marriage is procreation (Gen. 1:28), and Paul recommends marriage as a stop for immorality (1 Cor. 7:1–2, 9). As marriage is a type of Christ's relationship to the Church (Eph. 5:22), divorce is only permissible in the Bible in limited circumstances (Mal. 2:16; Matt. 5:31–32; 19:1–12; 1 Cor. 7:15). Marriage can be self-selected or arranged, and is a benefit and blessing to both parties. How can we have a biblical understanding of the covenant of marriage?

July 8: Parents

Parents are the paternal and/or maternal guardians responsible for raising their children. In the typical formation, a husband and a wife procreate to make children, and they then raise the children together as a father and a mother. But, oftentimes, individuals are left to raise their children alone, and some people become parents through adoption. Biblically, parents have certain obligations on how to raise their children. In the OT, the entire book of Proverbs is from Solomon teaching his son how to be a wise man, with wisdom personified as the ideal female figure. In the NT, Paul instructs fathers not to provoke their children to anger but to instruct them (Eph. 6:4; Col. 3:21) and for mothers to love them (Titus 2:4). How can we make sure we are godly parents?

July 9: Children

Children are the offspring of or adopted wards of parents. In the typical formation, a husband and a wife procreate to make children, and they then raise the children together as a father and a mother. But, oftentimes, parents adopt children who have been orphaned in order to raise them as their own. Biblically, children have obligations on how to treat their parents. The book of Proverbs was written largely by Solomon as an instruction book for his son on how to be wise, and wisdom is seen as the ideal woman. The Ten Commandments exhorts Israelites to honor their father and mother, and it is the only commandment with a promise, which is for a long life (Exod. 20:12; Deut. 5:16). This exhortation is continued in the NT (Eph. 6:1–3; Col. 3:20). Adoption is also a concept that is true of all believers in salvation (Eph. 1:5). How can we honor our parents?

July 10: Friendship

Friendship is the mutual relationship between two people who are not in a romantic or family relationship. Friendship is an important relationship in Scripture because it is a relationship that God can have with persons. Abraham is called God's friend (2 Chr. 20:7; Isa. 41:8; Jas. 2:23), and God spoke to Moses as a friend (Exod. 33:11). Jesus called the disciples His friends (John 15:13–14). There are many kinds of friendships. A strong example of friendship in the Bible is that of Saul's son Jonathan and King David (1 Sam. 17:57–18:1), even to the point of their making a covenant, which is not necessary in a friendship (1 Sam. 18:2–4; 20:42). These kinds of friendships are not based in what one can get out of it, like transactional relationships. There are also acquaintances, who are people we interact with regularly. What friendships do you have?

July 11: Work

Work is the process of fulfilling a task out of obligation and/or for compensation. God worked and established a Sabbath from it (Gen. 2:2–3; Exod. 20:8). He created man to work (Gen. 2:15, 18), but, since the Fall, work has been a toil (Gen. 3:17–19). In the OT, we are to work well (Eccl. 9:10), and not be vain in our work (Eccl. 2:22–25). In the NT, Christians are reminded not to grumble in work (Phil. 2:14–16), but we ought to contribute for ourselves and not depend upon others or steal (1 Thess. 4:11; 2 Thess. 3:10–12; Eph. 4:28). We also ought to be self-sufficient and not burden others. It is also important for us to know that, although we can be compensated, we work for God and our future reward (Col. 3:23–24). How is your attitude towards work?

July 12: Culture

A Culture is the combination of a peoples' language, arts, and customs that provide them a unique identity as a distinctive group. Cultures can be unique to a group, or they can change over time. In the Old Testament, there are aspects of Israel's culture that separate them as a unique people group in the ancient Near East (e.g., laws, religious practices, and language). Even though this is the case, there are also features that unite Israel with their neighboring cultures that make the ANE unique in its time and location compared to other cultures in different times and locations (e.g., livestock, food sources, and clothing). By the time of the New Testament, Israel's culture evolved in areas like language (Greek), money, and governance from their Assyrian, Babylonian, Persian, Greek, and Roman rulers. What are unique features in your culture?

July 13: Language

Language is spoken communication that has its own set of grammar and, typically, writing system. The Bible is written in three languages: Hebrew and Aramaic in the Old Testament and Greek in the New Testament. Biblically, separate languages began at the Tower of Babel (Gen. 11:1–9), and since then, have been unique to people groups. Because languages can range from being completely different systems to slightly different in dialect, languages can often separate groups into in-groups and out-groups. An example in the Bible is the "shibboleth" account in Judges 12:6. There are more than 7,000 languages today, and many more have existed in known history. What language(s) do you speak, and what languages would you like to learn?

July 14: Society

A Society is a large group of people within a particular area that have a shared culture, language, and government. The society that someone lives in is often the range of their experience and influence. Communities can be rural, suburban, and urban in their environment, larger or smaller in land area, and dense or sparsely populated. Many subcultures can make up a tapestry of different regional or ideological expressions within a society that can be experienced by all. In the NT, the cities were the cosmopolitan hubs of society, and churches were planted there due to the larger populations. This continues into the End Times, where the heavenly city is seen descending on Jerusalem. Here, all nations share the same culture of worshipping the Lord (Rev. 21). What are the things that make your society unique?

July 15: State

The State is a particular territory that has a unique culture and government uniting its citizens. The state is typically governed by an authority or multiple authorities that are either elected or have come to power by their efforts, lineage, or a military coup. There are usually authoritative laws that a state has that help rulers govern and establish order for the citizens of the state. These laws can be in a fixed law code or subject to change. A state can interact with different states in partnership or conflict as a unit, whether with mutual benefit or loss, or with individual benefit or loss. In Scripture, God establishes a territorial state for Israel (Gen. 15:18–21; Num. 34; Deut. 1:7), and peoples of every nation (state) will worship God in the End (Rev. 7:9), in a glorified new heavens and new earth. What makes your nation unique?

July 16: Ruler

The Ruler is the authority, leader, or sovereign of a state. Many kinds of rulers exist. A typical authoritarian ruler would be a king. A kingship can be passed along through a royal family line, through democratic vote, or through military force. In a modern democratic state, one can elect many kinds of rulers. In a parliamentary form of government, the majority party selects a prime minister who forms the government. In the American constitutional republican system, the citizens vote in an election with the Electoral College voting for the president. Because God is orderly, Christians are to be subject to their authorities (Rom. 13:1–7) except in cases of disobeying God (Dan. 3; 6; Acts 5:29). How can we be subject to rulers?

July 17: Forms of Government

A Form of Government is the system that a nation uses to maintain how a government operates in an orderly and repeatable manner. There are many forms of government, each with different philosophies underlying the reason that they operate how they do. *A Utopia is an idealistically perfect form of government*, and a *Dystopia is an idealistically imperfect form of government. Anarchy is a form of government with no rule*, and *Theocracy is a religious form of government. A Monarchy is a form of government with a monarch. A Democracy is a form of government that democratically elects its ruler. A Republic is a form of government where citizens elect representatives. Aristocracy, Oligarchy, and Timocracy are forms of government ruled by the powerful few.* What kind of form fits biblical principles?

July 18: Nationalism

Nationalism is a political ideology that puts a nation's focus primarily on its own interests. The primacy of a nation-state, or a view of the society and the state as a unit of focus, is often seen as a concern to those who espouse a more globalist perspective. This is in large part to the National Socialist (Nazi) party and their fascist allies in the early twentieth century with their ethno-nationalism and social Darwinism. But countries who often claim globalism as a view often have nationalist interests that betray a globalist perspective. In this way, it seems biblically-minded for citizens or a ruler to have their nation's best interest in mind, while also treating our global neighbors as beneficial partners when possible. How should Christians view nationalism in light of Scripture and history, knowing we are pilgrims in this land?

July 19: Globalism

Globalism is a political ideology that puts a nation's focus primarily on global interests. Globalism is a relatively recent phenomenon, as global travel has only been really possible since the 1500s, and the information age has only recently made global communication readily available. When considering global interests, one main topic of interest seems to be that of environmentalism. As debates about climate change have been intensifying, some question how nations can influence or legislate for mitigating the human contribution, if any, to climate change in the best interest for all national parties. For the Christian, the question is how can we, as citizens of particular nations, maintain our nation's interests and partner with other countries for mutual global benefit?

July 20: Immigration

Immigration is the process of becoming a citizen of another country. Every country has laws on how they deal with immigration. Often, a person or family emigrates, or travels to another country, to become a citizen of the country they come to. In this process, a person can become naturalized, or granted citizenship, if they follow the new country's procedures. After this, the person takes on the culture (acculturation) and national identity (assimilation) of that country. One may leave their country because they can positively benefit a country with their skills, they don't have as many opportunities in their original countries, or they are refugees fleeing harm. Biblically, Israel had laws on treating foreigners (Exod. 22:21; Lev. 19:9–10, 33–34), and Christians are pilgrims in this world (Heb. 11:13–16). How should we understand citizenship and immigration?

July 21: Economics

Economics is the study of the generation and transfer of wealth. Economics comes from the Greek terms *oikos* ("home") and *nomos* ("law"), and originally dealt with the management of the house. It has since come to refer to the financial realm of knowledge. Instead of guessing something's value when trading like goods for like goods in the barter system, people have developed currency with attributed values to them. This used to be exclusively in coinage by weight and metal type, which is why the Bible speaks of "honest weights and measures" (Deut. 25:15–16; Prov. 20:23), but banknotes, or paper currency, were later introduced to be a promised placeholder for what a bank has in its possession. How can we know and navigate economics?

July 22: Capitalism

Capitalism is an economic system where individuals own private property and exchange capital in a competitive free market system. Capital is anything of value that can be exchanged for other items of value. The concept of supply and demand is that people desire valuable things (demand) and others provide valuable things (supply). Capitalism is favorable towards *Supply Side Economics*, which *is a view that believes supplying more goods and services in the market benefits an economy.* Governments who favor the supply side wish to reduce taxes on businesses so they can produce. *Demand Side Economics is a view that believes increasing demand of goods and service in the market benefits and economy.* Keynesian Economists hold that governments should interfere with markets to increase demand. Is capitalism a biblical system?

July 23: Socialism

Socialism is an economic system where the society owns all labor production equally. Socialism was more formalized in the 1800s, although some form or another of it existed earlier. The atheist Karl Marx developed his form of socialism, called Marxism, where he argued that the lower economic class must rise up and seize wealth from the upper class in order to have equal distribution. From his works, governments adopted Communist forms of government, where a ruler ensures equal distribution of wealth for the society. Some sought to connect socialism with Christianity and developed liberation theologies, including Black Liberation Theology and Feminist Theology, which sought salvation through sociological equality, even by force. Is socialism a biblical system?

July 24: Rights

Rights are understood allowances, either from God or man, which are acknowledged by the state and received by citizens. Since the dawn of society, rulers have allowed their subjects to partake in the benefits of society at the ruler's mercy. Since the English Magna Carta (1215) the king's power was somewhat limited, and the later English Bill of Rights (1688/1689) acknowledged further civil rights for the people. In America, we acknowledge rights that cannot be infringed in our Bill of Rights, and inalienable, God-given rights of life, liberty, and the pursuit of happiness in the Declaration of Independence. In his "Letter from Birmingham Jail," Martin Luther King, Jr. appealed to laws being just or not in his pursuit of civil rights for all Americans. How can rights be inalienable or laws be objectively just or unjust without a just God above man?

July 25: War

War is the military conflict between two or more nations. Man is fallen and conflict is part of our sinful nature, and government is the natural extension of our desire for order in the Imago Dei. Therefore, governments run by men will have conflict with each other. The question is whether or not these military conflicts are Godly or not. In the OT, God explicitly sanctions some conflicts in Scripture (Deut. 7:2; 20; Josh. 6:2–5). But not every conflict in the Bible is of God. In the NT, Jesus gives many admonitions that seem to advocate for pacifism, or being in favor of no wars (Matt. 5:9, 39, 44; Luke 6:27). But Jesus said and will do things in the future to suggest Christianity is not a pacifist worldview (Matt. 10:34; 26:52; Rev. 19:15). With the canon being closed, how should we determine if wars are just today?

July 26: Slavery

Slavery is the ownership of a person and their labor. Slavery has been a negative part of many civilizations through history. People used to enslave people instead of killing them in war. In the OT, Israel had a debt-based slavery, where it was an option for debtors to serve as slaves, or choose to become a slave for better conditions. Slaves were released every 7 and 50 years (Lev. 25). Roman slavery was more brutal, not of God, and was usually reserved for non-Romans. The race-based Atlantic Slave Trade began with the Trans-Saharan Slave Trade, and was perpetuated by Muslims and then imperial Europe before ending with Christian abolitionists and the American Civil War. How can we fight slaveries that exist now, like human trafficking? *Ref.: Philemon*

July 27: Church and State

The connection of *Church and State is the question of how or if each institution should affect each other.* The union of the church and the state can take many forms. Countries like communist China or Nazi Germany can have a secular state that owns a state church that is subject to the edicts of the state. A theocracy, like the Roman Catholic Church in Vatican City or the Arabic countries that rule with sharia law, is the view that church should lead the state's decisions. The separation of church and state can take many forms, as well. The Eastern Orthodox view of symphonia is the separate but symbiotic relationship between the church and the state. The Jeffersonian view of the separation of church and state in his letter to the Danbury Baptist Association sees each institution separate from each other's jurisdiction. Which position do you hold to?

July 28: Canon Law

Canon Law is a law code that is governed by a particular church. In the OT, God provided a law code for Israel that met both civil and religious needs due to Israel being a theocracy. Because the church's heavenly citizenship, the authors of the New Testament never needed a civil law code. Since the legalization of Christianity in the late Roman Empire, there have been both civil laws within different European countries and canon laws maintained by various churches. Throughout the Middle Ages, the Roman Catholic Church began to codify their canon law, often with the power to punish citizens of different countries if these laws were broken. But canon laws do not exist for churches that do not have civil interests. How should Christians view canon law codes?

July 29: Civil Religion

A Civil Religion is the concept of a culture of religious practices, symbols, and myths that a nation observes overtly or implicitly. Originating from the French philosopher Jean-Jacques Rousseau, it can be argued that every country has a patriotic pride with a civil religion at its foundation. In the same way that a religion has a set of various beliefs, practices, and symbols, it is argued nations can share these qualities, as well. Symbols like a seal or a flag, founding myths like George Washington confessing to chopping down the cherry tree because he cannot lie, and practices like singing national anthems and participating in national holidays are all potential examples of civil religion. Any time Christians participate in worshipping the state, they are practicing a civil religion. How should Christians determine whether or not a civil religion a genuine concept?

July 30: Sects

A Sect is a distinct religious group or sub-group within a religion. Every world religion has different sects and denominations, and the Judeo-Christian religions are no different. Biblical Judaism can be roughly divided into the Ancient Israelite Religion of the OT, and the Second Temple Religion of the NT. Some Jewish sects that lived during the NT era are Pharisees, Sadducees, Essenes (possibly the Qumran Community), and the Zealots. The Church began to form groups during the life of the Apostles (1 Cor. 1:12; 3:4), but the Christian church has since developed official denominations. The Roman Catholic Church split from the Orthodox Church in 1054. The Protestant churches began in 1517, and there are now Lutherans, Anglicans, Calvinists, Baptists, Charismatic churches and more. How can we all be united in Christ?

July 31: Missiology

Missiology is the study of Christian missions and its movements. Missions began in the OT with Israel expected to have other nations come to God through them. But ever since Jesus gave the great commission (Matt. 28:16–20; Mark 16:14–18; Luke 24:44–49; John 20:21–23; Acts 1:4–8), Christians have gone and made disciples of all nations. Early on, the church went north into Europe, east to Asia, and south into Africa. With the advent of Islam in the Middle East and Africa, and in running into the long-established religions of Buddhism and Hinduism in Asia, Christianity mainly had a foothold in Europe. After Europe's experiment of imperialism throughout the world, global missions rose again in the nineteenth & twentieth centuries. How can we engage in and support missions?

August: Sin & Salvation

August 1: Hamartiology

Hamartiology is the study of sin, including its origin, nature, imputation, transmission, and effects. People of almost every worldview believe that humans can do bad things even if they disagree that people have a sin nature. From a biblical perspective, since the Fall, humans have had a sin nature in the same way that they have a physical nature. Because the Scriptures place a cosmic importance on morality, the reality of sin in the biblical worldview prompts some questions. One question is, if God is the good, and people were made good, how did evil come about? Another question is whether people actually have a sin nature at all. Also, how are sins determined? Hamartiology helps us understand how the Bible answers these questions. Have you ever thought about these questions?

August 2: Sin

Sin is the term for the ungodly nature from which persons commit negative actions. God is the only perfect and holy Being, and, therefore, He cannot sin. Alternatively, humans, being limited and imperfect, can choose against God and sin. Sin was not original to man, but we gained a sin nature in the Fall. Since then, it has affected the whole world. There are many terms in the Bible that refer to sin: not achieving goodness (sin) (Heb. *chata*; Grk. *hamartia*), evil/badness (Heb. *ra*; Grk. *kakos*, *poneros*), blame (*planao*), err (Heb. *shagag*), go astray (Heb. *taah* ; Grk. *paraptoma*); godlessness (Grk. *asebes*); guilt (Heb. *asham*; Grk. *enochos*), ignorance (Grk. *agnoein*), iniquity (Heb. *awon*), lawlessness (Grk. *anomia*), transgression (Heb. *pasha*; Grk. *parabates*), and unrighteousness (Heb. *rasha*; Grk. *adikia*). How can we see these categories in our own lives?

August 3: Chaos

Chaos is disorder which is not consistent with God. Although chaos is a common motif in the neighboring ancient Near Eastern cultures that surrounded Israel in the Old Testament, there is almost no mention of genuine chaos in the Bible. In the creation account in Genesis 1, where one might normally find chaos in ANE literature, we only find that the earth is "formless and void" (Gen. 1:2). This is also after the heavens and the earth were created, which means the earth was just primed for more order in the following days of creation. The real chaos in Scripture was after the Fall, where serpent, man, the earth because of him, and woman were all cursed. In the New Testament, we see that lawlessness, or inconsistency with God's order, is sin (1 John 3:4). How can we reflect God's order?

August 4: The Fall

The Fall is the starting point for sin on earth. Before the Fall, God considered all of creation as "good," and "very good" after humanity was created. God permitted Adam and Eve to eat any fruit of any tree in the garden except from the Tree of Knowledge of Good and Evil. In this way, God in His love provided an option for man in his free will to choose against God. The serpent spoke to and deceived Adam and Eve, and they freely chose to eat the fruit God commanded them not to eat. Because of this, death was introduced to humanity, men struggle with labor, women struggle in childbirth, and the sin entered into the world. This was the original sin that made people have a sin nature with the capacity to sin and need a solution to be in a right relationship with God. How do you see the effects of the Fall in your life?

August 5: Inherited Sin

Inherited Sin is the sin nature that is passed down from our ancestor Adam. Although the Fall was brought on humanity and the world by the original instance of sin, with Adam and Eve disobeying God and eating the fruit from the Tree of Knowledge of Good and Evil, inherited sin is often understood as original sin. This is because it is what all humanity receives from our ancestor Adam. Unlike imputed sin, inherited sin is passed down from person to person. It is through this inherited sin that all people experience effects on their nature and in spiritual death. Jesus defeated this sin on the cross and gives us new life in Him (2 Cor. 5:17; Gal. 2:20) through the Holy Spirit who we receive upon belief of the Gospel (John 20:31). How do we inherit Adam's sin?

August 6: Imputed Sin

Imputed Sin is the legal state of sin that humans have from God's perspective. In Romans 5:12–21, we are told that as sin entered the world through one man (Adam), and death entered through sin, so we all have sinned, and death passed to all men. One can commit a crime, but it is another thing to be declared guilty of that crime through a trial. Similarly, humans have a sin nature out of which they commit sins, but they also are considered guilty as sinners by God. Because of Adam's sin, all humans now have the same legal status that he received when he rebelled against God. In Christ, this imputed state can be annulled with the imputation of being declared righteousness by Christ. How can we live in light of our new declaration in Christ?

August 7: Transmission of Sin

The question for sin is how they get passed from Adam to us. *The Transmission of Sin is the process of sin being passed on from Adam to all people.* There is transmission of both our inherited sin and imputed sin. For imputed sin, all humans that ever existed receive their imputation directly from Adam. But there are many views on how inherited sin is passed down from person to person. In the past, Augustine of Hippo held to the *seminal view of transmission*, where *sin is passed down through human seed from the male line.* In this view, Mary's virginity is how Jesus was born sinless. In the Catholic doctrine of the Immaculate Conception, Mary was also born sinless through a miracle. A more biblical view is that inherited sin is spiritually received as individuals are created in conception. What is your view of the transmission of sin?

August 8: Depravity

Depravity is the term for the fallen state of man. Because of the clear need for salvation throughout the narrative of the Scripture, including the provision of Christ's death, burial, resurrection, and ascension, the depravity of humanity is apparent to all orthodox Christian sects. The question that divides Christians is to what extent humanity is depraved. Calvinists believe that humanity has *Total Depravity*, or *the belief that the effects of sin are to such a degree that people cannot and will not seek out salvation in their own efforts.* Other Protestant sects believe humans are depraved, but can still accept the gospel. Some, called Arminians, hold to a special, prevenient grace that enables the totally depraved to believe. Others merely believe total depravity does not hinder our ability to believe. How do you understand human depravity?

August 9: Effects of Sin

We can know that we are sinful, but what has sin done to us? *The Effects of Sin are the results humanity has due to the cause of inherited and imputed sin.* The primary effect of sin was the one God informed Adam and Eve of in the Garden, and that the Serpent twisted, which is spiritual death. There are many aspects of death that were introduced in the Fall, but spiritual death is the separation from God (Gen. 2:17; Rom. 5:12; 6:23). Other effects of sin are *Volitional Effects of sin*, or *the effects of sin on the will and all of its aspects.* This includes everything including our good and bad desires, including the societal consequences of sinful people interacting with one another. There are also the *Noetic Effects of sin*, which are *the effects of sin on the mind.* Some argue these effects make it so one cannot believe the Gospel. Do you see these effects in life?

August 10: Sins

Sins are the negative actions that humans commit from their sin nature. Temptation, or *being drawn to sin*, is not the same as sin (Jas. 1:14–15). We should know that the thought to sin is also a result of the Fall (Matt. 5:21–22, 27–28; 1 John 3:15). For committing sins, intentional sins are the most obvious. These are sins we commit knowing that they are sin. Of the intentional sins we commit, there are *Sins of Commission* or *committing bad deeds*, and *Sins of Omission*, or *intentionally not doing good things.* There are also unintentional sins. Although God's Law is written on our hearts (Rom. 2:15), we do not understand all morality, and, therefore, it is possible to commit an act without knowing it is immoral. What kinds of sins do you see in your life?

August 11: Degrees of Sin

Degrees of sin are levels of sin that are provided in Scripture. Although some sins can cause more harm than others in society, from God's perspective, sin is sin, and the consequence of sin is death. And although believers do not see condemnation (Rom. 8:1), all will face judgment (Rom. 14:10–11; Rev. 20:11–15). The famous seven deadly sins of envy, gluttony, greed, lust, pride, sloth, and wrath are an arbitrary, extra-biblical selection of sins, but there are seven detestable sins in Proverbs 6:16–19. Catholicism distinguishes between mortal, or damnable, sins, and venial, or not damnable, sins, but these categories are not biblical. There is also an unpardonable sin, which is to "blaspheme the Holy Spirit," although there is ambiguity as to what exactly this sin is. What degrees of sin do you see in the Bible?

August 12: Consequences of Sin

The Consequences of Sin are results one can receive from sins. Firstly, humanity will be judged for their actions in the End (Rom. 14:10–11; 2 Cor. 5:10; Rev. 20:11–15). But in this life, even for Christians, there are consequences for our sins. First, a regular problem is our loss of fellowship with the Lord, although this can be mended through confessing our sins to God (John 15:1–17; 1 John 1:9). In severe circumstances, we can become sick and even die (1 Cor. 11:30; 1 John 5:16). But even in this world, there are consequences for our sins that we observe, as we live in societies with laws that try to protect its citizens from others' sins. We can even experience relational consequences in this life from others who are on the receiving end of our sin. How have you experienced relational consequences for your sins?

August 13: Death

Death is the consequence of eating of the Tree of Knowledge of Good and Evil (Gen. 2:17), and it was introduced to the world after the Fall. Biblically speaking, *Death is severe separation.* There are three kinds of death in Scripture. The kind of death that is most apparent without special revelation is *Physical Death*, or *separation from our body and our spiritual self.* The next kind of death is *Spiritual Death*, or *the separation from God in this life.* As painful as physical death might be in our losing loved ones, spiritual death is painful for God, and all humanity struggles in life because of our lack of relationship with Him. The *Final Death*, or second death, *is eternal separation from God.* This is the death at the End for all those who are not with God in Christ, including death itself (1 Cor. 15:26; Rev. 20:11–15). How do you view death?

August 14: Soteriology

Soteriology is the study of the salvation of mankind, including its origin, means, and extent. There are many ways Christians have viewed man's salvation (*soteria*) since Christ's ascension. Strands of Christianity have prized a corpus of tradition, or historical, post-biblical testimony and non-canonical writings, on which to base their views of soteriology. There have also been many strands of Christianity who have focused on what the Scriptures have said about salvation, and they have chosen to base their soteriology on this data. Soteriology is a very important study in Christianity. If Scripture is God's very Word, it would make sense to begin there, and it can then be helpful after to see how others have viewed salvation. How do you study salvation?

August 15: Salvation

Salvation is the term used for all aspects of how Christians are cosmically rescued by God as laid out in Scripture. There are three main kinds of salvation in the New Testament: Justification is the Christian's initial salvation, sanctification is the Christians ongoing salvation, and glorification is the Christian's final salvation. There are also views of who is responsible for salvation. *Monergism is the view that God alone saves you and you can otherwise not choose salvation. Synergism is the view that God saves you once you freely choose to believe the gospel.* There is also the question of what you are saved from. We are certainly saved from the sin and death brought on by mankind in the Fall (John 3:16; Rom. 6:23; 1 Cor. 15:3–4), but we are also saved from God's wrath towards sin (Rom. 5:9; 1 Thess. 1:10). How do you view our salvation?

August 16: Ordo Salutis

Throughout the millennia of the church's existence, there has been a question amongst Christians as to the order of salvation. *The Ordo Salutis,* or order of salvation, *is the term for the order of the events that a person goes through on their journey in salvation.* The text for this doctrine is Romans 8:29–30. The chain of events listed are: foreknowledge, predestination, calling, justification, and glorification. The immediate issue with this chain is the lack of other aspects of salvation in the chain (e.g., election, regeneration, belief, etc.). Another issue is determining precisely when these events take place. Some have suggested that the list is not chronological, but that it could be a logical flow or merely a catalogue. How do you understand the order or salvation?

August 17: Foreknowledge

Foreknowledge is the timeless knowledge of God of certain events as understood by temporal humanity. The term *proginosko* simply means to know beforehand (fore, *pro;* know, *ginosko*), and, therefore, the term can be used to speak of when humans know things earlier in time (2 Pet. 3:17). For example, Paul's Jewish accusers knew of him as a Pharisee before he was an apostle (Acts 26:5). But because God knows all truth, there are many things in the Bible which God seems to know from beforehand, but in reality, He knows all from His timeless vantage point. God foreknew the Jews that He created in Abraham (Rom. 11:2). God also foreknew that Jesus would come and save mankind (1 Pet. 1:20). For the *Ordo Salutis,* Paul claims God foreknow those who would believe the Gospel. How do you see God's foreknowledge in the Bible?

August 18: Predestination

Predestination is the work of God of certain actions as understood by temporal humanity. From a human perspective, Paul gives an example of predestination (*proorizo*) as the Jews' and Romans' predetermination or premeditation of Jesus' crucifixion in Acts 4:28. But there are many things that God predestines to happen that are mentioned in the New Testament. In hindsight, the Gospel, which was once unknown in the Old Testament, is understood as predestined by Paul (1 Cor. 2:7). Paul also mentions that God predestined the adoption and inheritance of the Christian (Eph. 1:5, 11). When it comes to the *Ordo Salutis*, the Christian's being conformed to the image of the Son is predestined (Rom. 8:29–30). How do you see God's predestination in Scripture?

August 19: Election

Election is the selection of particular beings by God. Three groups of two types of beings are called "elect." Angels are elect (1 Tim. 5:21) and people. Of the groups of people, both Israel and the Church are called elect. As far as individuals in the NT, Paul speaks of a man named Rufus (Rom. 16:13) and John speaks of an elect lady (2 John 1:1, 13), which could be an individual or a particular church. The only other individual that is elect is Jesus, Himself (Isa. 42:1; Matt. 12:18–21; 1 Pet. 2:6), even mockingly (Luke 23:35). When election of Christians is not just stated, it is typically regarding something: holy and blameless (Eph. 1:4), obedience and Jesus' blood (1 Pet. 1:2). Whether election to salvation is corporate or individual, or conditional or unconditional are logical conclusions various theologians have made. How do you understand the election?

August 20: Atonement

The Atonement is the act of Jesus' reconciliation of man and God. Although sacrifices were commanded as placeholders in time, atonement actually only comes through the death of the God-man Jesus Christ and not through the sacrificial system (Isa. 1:11; Jer. 7:21–23; Heb. 10:4) (see *Death of Jesus*). There have been many views of the atonement: *Ransom, Christ pays for our release from Satan*; Christus Victor, *Christ is victorious against evil*; *Satisfaction, Jesus satisfies God's due honor*; *Moral Influence, Jesus' death moves us to love God*; *Governmental, Christ's death shows sin's cost;* and the protestant view, *Penal Substitution, Jesus takes our place.* Theologians question whether Jesus provided a *limited atonement*, or *reconciliation for a select few*, or an *unlimited atonement*, or *reconciliation for anyone*. Who is Christ's death for?

August 21: Grace

Grace is the unmerited favor that God gives to man. It is often said that mercy is not getting what you deserve, and grace is getting what you do not deserve. *Common Grace is unmerited favor given to all in God's provision of what is needed for life.* As for special, salvific grace, humanity is saved by grace through faith in Christ alone (Eph. 2:8–9), and there are many views of what grace is and whether it is something given to all people or not. Arminians believe that, because people are incapable of belief apart from God's work, they need *Prevenient Grace*, or *a special grace given to all men so that they are able to believe.* Calvinists believe in *Irresistible Grace*, or *special grace only for the elect that cannot be resisted.* Others believe in *Free Grace*, or *special grace freely given to all those who believe in Christ.* What view of grace do you hold?

August 22: Calling

Calling is a work of the Holy Spirit to bring people to salvation. Calling is a post-Pentecost ministry of the Holy Spirit (Gal. 4:6), and no one comes to God unless the Spirit draws them (John 6:44). Jesus tells his Israelite audience that "many are called, and few are chosen" (Matt. 20:16; 22:14). This helps make certain that calling and election are separate, but the question is how are we called? Non-Calvinist protestants believe that there is one, universal call to people, and Calvinists believe in two calls: a *General Call* where *God calls people to Christ through the preaching of the Scriptures* (Rom. 10:17; 1 Cor. 1:21), and an *Effectual Call* where *God calls the elect to Himself through the Holy Spirit.* No matter what, Christians are those people who have responded to the Spirit's calling. How has the Holy Spirit drawn you to Christ?

August 23: Belief

Belief is the positive human acceptance of the gospel by which people become Christians. A famous verse that discusses belief (*pisteuo*) is John 3:16, where Jesus speaks to Nicodemus, a member of the ruling class in Israel, about what he needs to believe to have life. John's Gospel is the only book of the NT written to unbelievers, and John states that his audience should "...believe that Jesus is the Christ, the Son of God" to have life in His name (John 20:31). Paul tells the Romans that the gospel is the power for salvation for everyone that believes it (Rom. 1:16). Some have presumed belief to be a work because it is something that humanity does, but belief is not a work because works cannot save mankind (Eph. 2:8–9; Gal. 2:16). When did you believe the gospel?

August 24: Regeneration

Regeneration is when a human is spiritually born new after believing the gospel. When Jesus spoke with Nicodemus, Jesus told Nicodemus that he must be born again (John 3:3). This was an odd statement to Nicodemus's ears, but it was also something that was unattainable until the ascended Jesus sent the Holy Spirit to humanity at Pentecost. Since then, people who accept the gospel are considered spiritually born again, born to incorruptible seed (1 Pet. 1:23), and new creations (2 Cor. 5:17) in this life as well as into eternal life (Rom. 6:23). This concept is also called regeneration and Paul speaks of regeneration as being washed and renewed by the Holy Spirit (Titus 3:5). Without being made new, it would be difficult to understand how the things of our newness in Christ can be applied to our old nature. How do you see being born again?

August 25: Reconciliation

Reconciliation is the renewed relationship that we have with God in Christ because of the atonement. Our right relationship with God in Christ is central to our salvation. The Bible provides examples of reconciliation in relationships between people who are angry with one another (Matt. 5:23–24) and reconciliation in marriage (1 Cor. 7:11). In our relationship with God, the Son took on a human nature to reconcile God and man (Heb. 2:17). Reconciliation is necessary, and it is the Christian's message to the world (2 Cor. 5:17–20). Through Jesus, God reconciled all men, both Jew and Gentile, to Himself (Eph. 2:14–16). Sinless Jesus took on all of humanity's sin so that God and humanity can be in right relationship (2 Cor. 5:21). How do you understand our reconciliation?

August 26: Adoption

Adoption is the doctrine that speaks of the sonship that Christians have in Christ in our relationship with God. There is little in Scripture that discusses Israelite adoption, but Roman adoption was powerful enough to impart family inheritances to those adopted into a family. Israel was a precursor of spiritual adoption, although through Abraham, the father of faith (Rom. 9:4; Gal 4:5). Christians are predestined for adoption (Eph. 1:5). In Christ, we are adopted as sons as opposed to being slaves to fear (Rom. 8:15–17). We also are not merely considered sons in a lesser sense, but we are considered co-heirs with Christ. Therefore, even though we are not sons the same way Christ is "the Son," we do receive His sonship in our new life in Him. How does taking on Christ's sonship strengthen your understanding of salvation?

August 27: Justification

Justification is the doctrine of the Christian's legally taking on of Christ's righteousness from God's perspective. Although humanity cannot have perfect righteousness in our nature, especially after the Fall, God alone is perfectly righteous. Therefore, mankind is both unable to make perfect decisions and is in need of gaining righteousness to be in relationship with God. Because Christ has a righteous character and flawless judgment, the Holy Spirit is able to impute His righteousness to us upon belief (2 Cor. 5:21), making us declared righteous in God's sight (Rom. 5:1). Although we can make godly determinations and actions now through the Spirit, when we are glorified, our righteousness will be perfect (1 Co. 6:3). How do you view our righteousness?

August 28: Eternal Security

Eternal Security is the doctrine regarding the Christian's permanence in their salvation. Throughout the various Christian denominations, there are only two ways one can understand salvation: permanent or contingent. For the Arminian sects, they believe that Christians can lose their salvation. They see the warning signs in the book of Hebrews not as losing fellowship, but losing salvation (e.g., Heb. 5:11–6:20). The Calvinist response to this is *Perseverance of the Saints*, or *the view that if you are elect, you will persevere to the end.* Some have attempted to agree to *Preservation of the Saints*, or *the view that if you are elect, God will preserve you to the end.* Others hold to the doctrine of *Once Saved, Always Saved* (OSAS), or *the belief that once someone accepts the Gospel, they are saved for life.* What is your view of eternal security?

August 29: Sanctification

We read in the *Ordo Salutis* that those who are justified are also glorified (Rom. 8:30). This means that those who experience the initial aspect of salvation will also go to heaven, which is the last aspect of salvation. The question is, what about salvation during the Christian's day-to-day life? *Sanctification is the doctrine of the Christian's continually conforming to the image of Christ for holiness.* Because we navigate the world through our actions, we may presume that we contribute to our salvation. But sanctification is a perfect work of Christ (1 Thess. 5:23) provided through Christ's sacrifice (Heb. 10:14). It is also something that will be completed by Christ (Phil. 1:6). Christians are sanctified by God through His Word (John 17:17). How do you understand the doctrine of sanctification in your life?

August 30: Repentance

Repentance is the doctrine where we reject sin in favor of God's truth. Repentance is important because it is a prime reason for the Protestant Reformation. The Greek term for repentance, *metanoia*, was translated in the Latin Vulgate into *Penance*, or *taking action to pay for past sin*. These included *Indulgences*, or *ways to buy fewer penalties in the afterlife.* The Reformer Martin Luther posted his *95 Theses* in response to this misreading. Biblically, John the Baptist's repentance was for the nation of Israel to acknowledge Jesus as their Messiah and King (Matt. 3:2; 4:17). There is a debate as to whether repentance is necessary for salvation, or whether it is a work that humanity can do apart from God's work in salvation. No matter how repentance is viewed, it is expected in some way from the Christian (2 Pet. 3:9). How do you view repentance?

August 31: Glorification

Glorification is the final state of salvation that affects the whole person, body and soul. We read in the *Ordo Salutis* that those who are justified are also glorified (Rom. 8:30). This means that those who experience the initial aspect of salvation will also go to heaven. Jesus is the example of glorification, as He is glorified first of all mankind, and we can read about how His glorified body operates in the Scriptures. We see that Jesus is not merely His divine nature after His resurrection, but He maintains His human nature forever as well (Heb. 1:3). As normally expected from a human, we see Jesus can eat and be touched, but He can also appear at will (John 20–21). We are told that, like Jesus, we will have incorruptible, physical bodies in the End (1 Cor. 15:42–57). How does glory give you joy?

September: Creation

September 1: Creation

Creation is the doctrine that speaks to both spiritual and physical reality and time and God's act of creating them. Every worldview has an understanding of how everything came to be. In early polytheistic religions, the various gods created out of existing materials, including themselves. In atheistic naturalism, a Big Bang event brought about all matter and time that has been randomly changing ever since. In the Judeo-Christian Scriptures, God spoke everything into existence in the six days of creation written about in Genesis 1. How that passage ought to be interpreted has been understood differently by Christians throughout the years. But all Christians hold to God's creating of all spiritual and material creation. How can we take the biblical and scientific data and arrive at faithful conclusions?

September 2: Cosmological Argument

The Cosmological Argument is the argument for God's existence from the necessity for a first cause for the universe. This argument was first formulated by Islamic scholars, but has since been argued by Christian theologians. The argument has been formulated many ways, but it generally states that a "Prime Mover" must have created the cosmos because it began at some point in time and space, and only God is outside time and space. Because the universe is material and temporal, whatever caused it must be immaterial and atemporal. Those options are inanimate objects (concepts like shapes and numbers) and minds. Because inanimate objects cannot create, that leaves a mind as the only possibility. Christians would argue this immaterial and atemporal mind that created is God. Do you agree with this?

September 3: Teleological Argument

The Teleological Argument is the argument for God's existence from the order of the cosmos. The argument's logical formation is tHis: The order of the universe to permit life on this earth could only come from and intelligent designer. Neither necessity nor chance can explain order and life. If the orderliness of the universe was out of necessity, there could be no other possibilities of how the universe could be. But there are endless possibilities of how this universe could have ended up, and, therefore, necessity does not explain how we got here. If chance, given the larger percentage of chance that the universe did not permit life, it is far more probable than not that the universe would not permit order and life. Therefore, design is the best explanation for life in the universe. And if design is the most logical solution, who could be that designer?

September 4: Intelligent Design

Intelligent Design is the argument that the created world around us shows examples of order and design which necessitates a personal divine mind. Since the Enlightenment, many philosophers and scientists have sought to provide naturalistic arguments for the questions of the origin of matter from no matter, life from non-life, and humanity non-humanity. In the course of time, no physical explanations have been able to answer these questions. Some in modernity have attempted to explain how the traditional view of a deity can answer these questions. Critics of intelligent design have called Godly explanations "God of the gaps" arguments, but God could guide discoverable, natural means argued by naturalists. Can God be the designer?

September 5: Young Earth Theory

The Young Earth Theory is the view that the earth is only about 6,000 years old. The youngness of the earth in this view is based on how the years in the Scriptures can be calculated if interpreted literally. A view that is almost synonymous with the Young Earth position is the *Literal 24-Hour View*, or that *the days that make up the creation week each took 24 hours.* This view is often held by those who hold to a historical-grammatical interpretation of Scripture. Inspired biblical testimony is also prized over scientific consensus by holders of this view. The justification for biblical favoritism is that the Bible is God's actual Word and scientific consensus is subject to change upon new data. Scientific data is useful, but only in results of our current understanding. Can those sympathetic to scientific conclusions hold this view?

September 6: Day-Age Theory

Some have held to the day-age theory to try to be more faithful to the scientific data. *The Day-Age Theory is the theory of creation where each "day" of the creation week is actually a long period of time.* In this way, one could read everything about the creation account literally, only the days mentioned can be understood as the long periods of time that scientists suggest is needed for the appearance of an old earth. This view holds an *Old Earth View*, or the view that *God created the earth billions of years ago or appearing to be that old*. The question comes down to whether the word for "day" (*yom*) should be understood as literal days or periods of time. To God, a day is a thousand years, but this seems to be referring to his timelessness (2 Pet. 3:8). How do you understand "day" in Genesis 1?

September 7: Gap Theory

The Gap Theory is the belief that there is an extended period of time before the literal week of creation. This is another Old Earth view of creation that seeks to reconcile the literal account of Genesis 1 with the scientific consensus of an old cosmos. In order to be faithful to the Bible, the days in the creation week are viewed as 24-hour days. But, in order to arrive at the old Earth view, there is an extended period of time between God's creation of the heavens and earth in verse 1 and the ordering of the earth and cosmos in the rest of the creation account. Although this view can be held without disrupting the flow of Genesis 1, there is no textual account for the placement of this time period into the creation week. Therefore, although one could hold this view, it is an argument from silence. What is the best way to reconcile the biblical and scientific accounts?

September 8: Big Bang Theory

The Big Bang theory is the view that the matter and time that make up the cosmos were brought about by a singular and physical event apart from supernatural means. Because infinite regress is logically and physically impossible and the universe appears to be expanding, physicists and astronomers began to hypothesize an event where matter and time began. Because this theory is intended, in part, to explain the origin of time, the moment this even occurs is T=1, and anything happening prior to this event is called T=0. An issue with this view is that it still struggles with the problem of infinite regress, as one can ask where did the Big Bang come from? And what immaterial and atemporal substance pre-existed matter and time to produce matter and time?

September 9: Multiverse Theory

The Multiverse Theory is the view that proposes that there are multiple parallel universes and this one happens to be the one that is life-permitting. The reason that some may hold this hypothesis is the overwhelming probability that the universe seems designed for life, particularly on earth. Multiverse theorists argue that if one takes the same overwhelming statistics of probability that the universe was fine-tuned for life and, instead, presume that there are the same number of universes, that our universe can be the one in a potentially innumerable amount that can produce life. The issue with this view as an argument against intelligent design is that if God can explain the existence of one universe, He must create all potential universes for the same reasons. Is it even possible to explain fine-tuning apart from and intelligent designer?

September 10: Simulation Theory

Simulation Theory is the view that the universe that we experience is an advanced generated program. The philosopher Rene Descartes is known for questioning his senses so much that he doubted his own existence. When he considered his pondering, he concluded, "I think, therefore, I am." This has caused others to propose the problem, of whether we are not just a brain in a jar being fooled to think we are experiencing life. Simulation theory is an extension of this problem. If we can make computers so advanced that we cannot tell their graphics from real life, how do we know someone has not trapped us in this program? People use this as a rationale to explain fine-tuning. The question is the same for the physical world, who created the simulation? Then, who made the physical world the simulation is in?

September 11: Ex Materia

Ex Materia is the view that the cosmos was made from pre-existing material. The modern scientific and the ancient Greco-Roman views on how the cosmos came to be have similarities. The ancient thinkers only had two types of generation to base creation off of: physical procreation of humans and animals and craftsmanship of goods from materials (wood, clay, etc.). Therefore, it is not a surprise that Hesiod's *Theogony* and Ovid's *Metamorphoses*, the primary sources for Greek and Roman creation respectively, both speak of gods creating from themselves and other materials. Today, because science can only consider existing matter and time in its hypotheses, there must be some kind of infinite regress without God. How else could everything come about?

September 12: Ex Nihilo

Ex Nihilo is the view that the cosmos was made by God from nothing but His will. Because of the problem of *infinite regress*, or *the perpetual existence of material and time into infinity past*, there is a problem in any purely scientific explanation for matter coming from non-matter. But unlike the modern scientific hypotheses and the procreation explanations from the ancient world, the explanation of God creating in Genesis 1 has Him creating without preexisting materials. God speaks into existence the formless and void earth, then light, and then, after shaping the realms of the cosmos, He populates those realms by speaking stars, plants, and creatures into existence. Although this initially is a miraculous, theological explanation for creation, it bypasses the scientific problem of infinite regress. Does God's creation ex nihilo help your faith?

September 13: The Heavens and the Earth

The Heavens and the Earth is the term for the cosmos in general in Genesis 1. In Genesis 1, we are told, "In the beginning, God created the heavens and the earth." In the modern disciplines of physics and philosophy, *Cosmology is the study of the cosmos. Cosmogony is the term for the origin of the cosmos*, and it is a sub-discipline of cosmology. Science can only use material and time for its experimentation, so philosophy is needed for seeing alternative explanations outside of these building blocks. Although the ancients did not have the advancement of physics or experience in using satellites to examine the solar system, there was still much interest in the ancient world in our universe. How can we use science and Scripture to understand our cosmos?

September 14: The Waters

The Waters is the term for all things having to do with water in Genesis 1. Water seems to be a part of the initial creation of the heavens and the earth, as "the Spirit of God moved upon the face of the waters" in the earth's formless and void state (Gen. 1:2). In modernity, *Hydrology is the study of water.* In Genesis, water is separated into the waters on the earth and the "firmament" in the air. *Firmament is the term for an ancient understanding of a dome over the earth, in this case of water.* This is close to our understanding of the atmosphere regarding the water cycle. Next, God separates the waters from dry land, creating the earth's oceans. *Oceanography is the term for the study of the oceans.* In the creation account, we see these realms of water separated with the further intention to house life. How is water understood theologically in the Scriptures?

September 15: Land

Land was formed in the beginning and was formed by God separating the waters on the third day in Genesis 1. In modern times, *Geology is the study of the earth.* Regarding territories, *Geography is the study of the natural features and political boundaries of the earth.* In the ancient world, there are many terms for various landmasses, but outside of description, it seems like the peoples of Scripture were primarily interested in *Cosmic Geography*, or *the belief of spiritual boundaries of the earth.* These include gardens (e.g., the Garden of Eden) and mountains (e.g., Mt. Sinai) being owned by God or spirits (Dan. 10:13). If the flood account in Genesis is global, then we cannot be sure of what the land looked like prior to that. How can we view land theologically?

September 16: Plant Life

Plant Life is all the seed-bearing vegetation created in Genesis 1. Plants first appear in the creation account with the separation of water to create dry land on the third day (Gen. 1:9–13). Here, the plant life is seed-bearing and able to produce fruit. Although Adam is created on the sixth day of creation (Gen. 1:26–31), in Genesis 2:5, humanity is on the earth before every plant and herb of the field. This can simply be before the plants were either germinated or cultivated. *Botany is the term for the modern study of plant life.* The current scientific consensus of when multicellular plant life began on earth is about 400 million years after multicellular animals. Plants have important meaning biblically in garden imagery in the temple and in illustrations of fruit production. How else do plants play a role in the Bible theologically?

September 17: The Stars

The Stars in the creation account of Genesis 1 is at least referring to the celestial bodies in the universe, if not also angelic beings. It could be that angels were created the same day as the stars. Interestingly, light pre-existed the sun, moon, and stars in creation (Gen. 1:3, 14–19), and light will exist in the End apart from the celestial bodies (Rev. 21:23). This light was originally sourced in God Himself, giving us a glimpse of how His glory may be. Like many ancient societies around the world, scholars of the ancient Near East studied the stars with great interest. Although they are vastly different studies today, the disciplines of astronomy and astrology were combined in the ancient world. *Astronomy is the scientific study of the stars* and *Astrology is the study of the stars for spiritual purposes.* Can biblical astrology exist?

September 18: Birds and Fish

Birds and Fish are the creatures that were created on day 5 and that occupy the realms of the sea and the sky in the creation account of Genesis 1. Ichthyology is the scientific study of fish, and *Ornithology is the scientific study of birds*. Both of these creatures play significant roles in the Scriptures. There are clean and unclean birds and fish in the Law. The dove is a bird used in Levitical sacrifices, and the quail was a food source for the Israelites in their wanderings in the wilderness. The fish plays a role in the OT with the great fish that rescues Jonah being a type for Jesus' burial. There are also many passages about fishing in the Gospels, often as examples of provision (Matt. 13:47–50; 17:24–27; Mark 6:35–44; 8:1–10; Luke 5:6; John 21:5–6). How can we consider birds and fish from a theological point of view?

September 19: Animals

Animals came from the earth on the fifth day of creation in Genesis 1 and are creatures that occupy the realm of the dry land. Living creatures, like man, were brought forth from the earth instead of being created from nothing (Gen. 1:24). The broad categories of livestock (*behemah*), creeping things (*remes*), and wild animals, or beasts of the earth (*chay erets*) are mentioned in Genesis 1:24–25, demonstrating an early understanding of classification. In modern times, *Biology is the study of life*, and *Zoology is the study of animal life*. In these disciplines, we classify creatures in the categories of domain, kingdom, phylum, class, order, family, genus, and species, now having a far more detailed categorization of animals. Taxonomy is either grounded in or can critique evolutionary theory. Do you believe we will see animals in the afterlife?

September 20: Dinosaurs

How do dinosaurs fit into the creation account? *Dinosaurs are large, reptile-like creatures that lived on the earth in the past but have gone extinct*. In modern times, *Paleontology is the study of dinosaurs and their fossils*. Depending on one's view, one holds an old earth view and believes the scientific view of dinosaurs dying off millions of years ago, or one holds a young earth view and believes the dinosaurs died in and shortly after the flood account in Genesis 6–9. The young earth view would argue that most of the fossils we have today are preserved by being rapidly buried in mud show great demonstration for the flood's role in the fall of the dinosaurs. Some argue these could be the dragons from the stories of the ancients. What is your view of the dinosaurs?

September 21: Creation of Man

The Creation of Man took place on the sixth day of the creation account in Genesis 1. In the biblical account of creation, humanity was created first through Adam by the dust of the earth and the breath of God (Gen. 2:7). A common way to address all humans, male or female, is by the masculine title "man" or "mankind." This does not mean that there are no differences between man and woman. Unlike women, men have masculine attributes, if not masculine roles, as well. *Masculinity is the concept that there are certain qualities of humanity that are exclusive to male persons.* As a whole, humanity is unique in creation as they are made in the image of God. Mankind is also commanded to multiply, and they are responsible for taking care of the rest of creation (Gen. 1:28). What does biblical masculinity look like to you?

September 22: Creation of Woman

The Creation of Woman took place on the sixth day of the creation account in Genesis 1. In Genesis 2:18–25, woman was created to help man. Eve was created from one of Adam's ribs after God put him to sleep. *Femininity is the concept that there are certain qualities of humanity that are exclusive to female persons.* This is different than *Feminism*, or *the belief that women should have certain rights not granted to them in a male-dominated society.* Different waves of feminism either accepted or rejected by modern society include voting rights, employment, and liberation from patriarchy. Christians can hold to two views of gender roles: *Complementarians believe in gender roles, Egalitarians do not believe in gender roles.* What position do you hold?

September 23: Abiogenesis

Abiogenesis is the view that all life on earth came from non-living matter. This is the view largely held by naturalistic atheists and the scientific community. There is no dominant view for how this life coming from non-life occurred, but there are some theories that have been proposed. One of these non-theistic theories is that there could have been a "primordial soup" of sorts, where non-living matter was brought to life in a pool of certain elements that produced the right, unknown combination to begin life. Another view is that life outside of earth seeded life on earth via panspermia (see *Exotheology*). These views do not answer the question of life from non-life in a satisfying way, but scientists continue to search for the answer through abiogenesis. How should Christians view the theory of abiogenesis?

September 24: Polygenesis

Polygenesis is the view that humanity originated from many sources. In this view, modern humanity (*homo sapiens*) came from many hominid ancestors. The result would be *Polyphylogeny*, or *the view that a group that makes up a species has a mixture of different kinds at different stages of evolution.* This has seen scrutiny because, if humanity had many kinds of "sub-human" ancestors, some *homo sapiens* could be more or less evolved. This view can, and has, bolstered prejudice that some "races" are more advanced than others. If true, one would have to argue how supremacists or eugenicists that wanted to praise or purify *homo sapiens* DNA were wrong. One would also have to state when apes end and humanity begins. How is this view unbiblical?

September 25: Monogenesis

Monogenesis is the view that humanity originated from one source. This view is the view of human origins that is held by most Christians, and it is the most faithful position given the biblical data. Here, one would argue that God created Adam and Eve as the first humans, and all the rest of humanity has come from these two ancestors. This could be from *Monophylogeny*, or *the view that a group that makes up a species is from one kind evolutionarily.* In this view, there are no more or less evolved people, only people who have adapted slight differences throughout the world. A problem with this view is the many examples of hominid fossils that would seem to suggest an evolutionary tree of humanity ultimately descending from apes. How can those who hold to monogenesis answer this?

September 26: Naturalistic Evolution

Naturalistic Evolution is the view that all living organisms evolved from a single common ancestor through the process of random mutation. Although there are some concepts of naturalistic evolution that predate him, the person who is credited with developing this theory is the British naturalist Charles Darwin. In fact, Darwinian Evolution is another common name for this theory. In this view, biologists look at the various species on earth and speculate a multitude of transitional species that connect all living organisms on earth with various tree-like models. Many biologists, including Darwin, himself, have issues with this theory. One is the concept of *Irreducible Complexity*, or *the idea that some biological systems cannot have evolved from simpler systems.* Why is the naturalistic evolutionary view incompatible with Christianity?

September 27: Theistic Evolution

Theistic Evolution is the view that all living organisms evolved from a single common ancestor through God's guiding of mutations. For some Christians, the evidence for Darwinian evolution is undeniable, and the research of biologists is trusted to find potential solutions to the issues of evolutionary theory. Because theistic evolution relies on the same basic premises as naturalistic evolution, the same problems follow this view. In addition to the problem of transitional species and irreducible complexity, theistic evolution also must embrace the harshness and need for suffering, and the seeming bias of God to preserve some species and let others go extinct. The issue that Christians often have with the theory is the presumption that mutations can produce order. Why would God guide the evolutionary process?

September 28: Descent of Man

The Descent of Man is the common term for the evolution of man through hominins from apes. The term was popularized by Charles Darwin from his book of the same name. There have been many fossils attributed to hominins since the theory of evolution was proposed, and there have been many models of how this descent could have happened. So far, it is generally argued that *homo heidelbergensis* came from *homo erectus*. From there, Neanderthals and Denisovans are precursors to the modern man, *homo sapiens*. Although attempts have been made to trace the evolution of man, it is unclear when man came from non-man, and this is still a problem for those that hold to macro evolution. The question for Christians is how can one classify humanity and sin in the descent of man?

September 29: Y-Chromosomal Adam

Y-Chromosomal Adam is the term for a singular individual in the past that all people now descend from genetically. There is a distinction between a genealogical Adam and a genetic Adam. The Bible is concerned with *Genealogy*, or *the tracing ancestry through family trees. Genetics is the study of tracing one's genetic ancestry.* One can find a Y-Chromosomal Adam in genetic history, but this is not the same as finding the first human that all of humanity comes from. There has been advancement in understanding genetics from the *Human Genome Project, a project that sought to find the base pairs of the DNA of humanity*, but there are still questions regarding the origin of man that has yet to be discovered. Could we discover a genetic Adam for human origins?

September 30: Mitochondrial Eve

Mitochondrial Eve is the term for a singular individual in the past that is the source of all mitochondrial DNA. When looking at human genetics, *Mitochondrial DNA is the genetic information is passed down exclusively from females.* When looking at human origins, there is the concept of a mitochondrial Eve that all humans can trace their genetic ancestry from. A problem with this genetic ancestor is that the mitochondrial Eve and the y-chromosomal Adam live thousands of years apart, making these two incompatible for a true historical Adam and Eve. There is hope that, because we can trace human origins to specific genetic ancestors, we can potentially find a genetic pair for human origins. But, is it more important that we understand that the biblical, genealogical ancestors Adam and Eve are the origin of humanity?

October: End Times

October 1: Eschatology

Eschatology is the study of the End Times, including what events take place in the End and when those events take place. Eschatology can often be a divisive topic within Christian theology for many reasons. First, throughout the history of the Church, many other doctrines took priority, like the Trinity and hypostatic union in the first centuries and the question of soteriology during the Reformation. Some of the dominant eschatological views were not debated until the seventeenth and nineteenth centuries. Second, there are interpretative methods that underlie certain eschatological views. Finally, people may have bitter disagreements because conversations revolve around our eternity with God. How can we interpret End Times properly?

October 2: Protoevangelium

The Protoevangelium is the very first prophecy about mankind's ultimate salvation found in Genesis 3:15. After the Fall, God curses the serpent, woman, and man. Within this series of curses, God provides hope in His curse of the serpent. Here, He speaks about putting enmity between the serpent's "seed" and the "seed of the woman." This statement is biologically incorrect for the woman, as the female carries the egg, not the seed. But this could be referring to Jesus, who was born of a virgin. God also states that the serpent's seed will "bruise his heel," possibly talking about Satan's false victory at the cross due to Jesus' saving mankind and rising from the dead. God proclaims Satan's eventual demise by saying the seed of the woman will "bruise [the seed of the serpent's] head." Can this prophecy embolden our faith in God's plan?

October 3: Reincarnation

Reincarnation is the belief that one returns to life in another form after they die depending on the good or bad that they have done in life. Different worldviews have believed in reincarnation, but the Eastern worldviews of Hinduism and Buddhism are the predominant religions that still hold this view today. Reincarnation is grounded in *Karma*, or *the view that what you do in this life will affect what happens to you in the life to come.* This moral framework determines whether one will come back as a lesser creature after death or either move closer to finally becoming one with everything, which is the predominant view of god in Hinduism, or move closer to lack of existence in Buddhism. Can this view be held by Christians given Heaven and Hell?

October 4: Nirvana

Nirvana is the extinguishing of self and suffering at the ultimate end of the karmic cycle in Buddhism. Buddhists continue the belief of reincarnation in the karmic cycle from Hinduism. The path toward Nirvana in Buddhism, however, begins with *Enlightenment*, or *the Buddhist belief of a cosmic awakening that life is suffering.* According to Buddhism, Siddhartha Gautama, a rich, Hindu prince, was sheltered in a palace, and, when he was exposed to the suffering outside the palace walls, meditated under a tree and reached enlightenment. The primary driver in Buddhism is suffering, and that is why, instead of becoming part of the reality that suffering comes from, Buddhists desire to ultimately cease by escaping existence. For the Christian, how should we view suffering knowing the God-man Jesus Christ endured it for us?

October 5: Annihilationism

Annihilationism is the view that unbelievers will not suffer in Hell for eternity, but will cease to exist after death. This view is largely held by Jehovah's Witnesses and Seventh-Day Adventists, but a minority of Evangelicals have begun to hold this view, as well. The adherents of this view juxtapose it with what they call *Eternal Conscious Torment* (ECT), or *the historically orthodox view that unbelievers go to Hell when they die.* The reasons typically offered for annihilationism are not necessarily grounded in the biblical data, which speaks of Hell often, but from the grounds of God's loving character. The question that should be asked in light of the biblical data is, why is Hell even referenced and contrasted with Heaven if it is not an option? *Ref.: Matt. 7:21; 1 Cor. 6:9–10; Rev. 20:15; 21:8*

October 6: Futurism

Futurism is the view that believes the events in eschatological texts will take place in the future. In the book of Revelation, there are many events that take place that require interpretation and categorization. In this interpretive framework, the tribulation, millennial kingdom, and the final states of heaven and hell are all events that will take place at some time in the future. One reason to hold this view is that apocalyptic literature, the genre of literature that the book of Revelation is written in, tends to be forward looking in its makeup. Another reason that some hold this view is that certain prophecies in the Old Testament have not yet taken place, and, therefore, there is still need for future fulfillment. Because of this, futurists continue to look forward to future events with hope and, typically, pessimism. Do you hold a futurist position? Why?

October 7: Preterism

Preterism is the view that believes the events in eschatological texts already took place within or near biblical history. In the book of Revelation, there are many events that require interpretation and categorization. In this interpretive framework, the tribulation and the millennial kingdom are events that already took place. One example is that the books of Daniel and Revelation speak about the destruction of Jerusalem and the Temple as the events that make up the tribulation. It is also typical in this view that we are already in the "millennial kingdom," which is not necessarily a literal timeline of one thousand years, but the time between Jesus' ascension and His return. Do you believe that preterism is the best framework for eschatology? Why?

October 8: Historicism

Historicism is the view that believes the events in eschatological texts have taken place from the completion of the Bible to Christ's second coming. In the book of Revelation, there are many events that take place that require interpretation and categorization. In this interpretive framework, the events that make up the tribulation, including the various judgments of seals, trumpets, and bowls, and the individuals like the beast, the harlot, and the antichrist, are all events and persons with actual historical representations. Some early protestant formations of this view have a majority of the events and persons fitting in with Catholicism, seeing atrocities and popes filling these prophecies. Even though they see the tribulation in historical events, historicists still look forward to a millennial kingdom. Can one clearly classify the tribulation historically?

October 9: Idealism

Idealism is the view that believes the events in eschatological texts are to be understood symbolically as timeless principles. In the book of Revelation, there are many events that require interpretation and categorization. In this interpretive framework, the tribulation, millennial kingdom, and even the final states of heaven and hell are all symbols that represent themselves in the human experience. The tribulation can represent the human struggle on earth, especially for Christians. The millennial kingdom can be seem as Christ's current reign in the Church. Heaven and hell can be representations for simply being with or without Christ based on the decisions we do in life. If idealism is right, what would be the consensus amongst holders of this view?

October 10: The Intermediate State

The Intermediate State is the term for the experience of humanity after physical death but before Jesus' second coming. Because of the Fall, all people experience physical death. Paul teaches that to be absent with the body is to be present with the Lord (2 Cor. 5:8). This means that upon physical death, the Christian is to be with Jesus. We also see that, regardless of one's eschatological view, Jesus has not returned again like we see in either the Rapture (1 Thess. 4:13–17) or other texts that speak of our future glorification (1 Cor. 15:51–52; Phil. 3:20–21). Therefore, there is a time between death and our glorification. The question is, what does state that look like? Because we neither have a physical body nor an incorruptible body until the end, only our souls must be with Jesus when we die unless we are unsaved. How do you understand this state?

October 11: The Second Coming

The Second Coming is the coming of Jesus to Earth after His ascension. In the Gospels and Acts, we see Jesus' ascension as He goes to be with the Father in heaven, but not before He told the disciples that He would return one day (John 14:3). There are generally a couple beliefs regarding Jesus' second coming. The first is that all Christians see Jesus finally coming back after the Tribulation (Rev. 19:11–21). For those that hold to the rapture of the Church (1 Thess. 4:13–17), they would believe Jesus first comes back to collect believers before, during, or after the Tribulation. The second coming of Jesus is important in Christian theology because it matters if Jesus' testimony and triumph, as well as the Scripture's prophesying, comes to pass. How can we have sure hope in Jesus' return?

October 12: The Rapture

The Rapture is the doctrine that speaks of Jesus' collecting the living and dead church before, during, or after the Tribulation. Depending on one's eschatological framework, the Rapture is either a relatively new view (1800s) or a forgotten doctrine of the Church taught by Paul in the NT. This idea is from Paul's encouragement to the church in Thessalonica, telling them they will see those Christians who died in persecution resurrected again before the End (1 Thess. 4:13–17). After this resurrection, both dead and alive Christians will be "caught up" in the clouds with Jesus. There are several views of the rapture: before the Tribulation (Pretribulation), in the middle of the Tribulation (Midtribulation), after the sixth seal (Mid-Wrath), after the Tribulation (Posttribulation) or a Partial Rapture for faithful Christians. Do you believe in the Rapture?

October 13: Day of the Lord

The Day of the Lord is the prophesied time of God's expended wrath on the various nations of the world. The term is mentioned in the prophets for a time of judgment on the enemies of Israel (Isa. 2:12; 7:18–25; 13:6, 9; Ezek. 30:3; Joel 1:15; 2:1, 11, 31; 1 Cor. 5:5). It a time of darkness (Amos 5:18, 20), it is near and comes like a thief in the night (Joel 3:14; Obad. 1:15; Zeph. 1:7, 14; Zech. 14:1; 1 Thess. 5:2; 2 Thess. 2:2; 2 Pet. 3:10), and there will be a battle (Ezek. 13:5), which we see as the Battle of Armageddon (*har megiddo* = Mount of Megiddo) (Rev. 16:14–16). Elijah will come before the Day of the Lord (Mal. 4:5). This term seems to represent both the Tribulation in general and the Battle of Armageddon together. Where do you think Christians will be in this day?

October 14: The Seventy Weeks

The Seventy Weeks are a period of time prophesied by Daniel that contains a series of troubles. The concept comes from the ninth chapter of Daniel, specifically Daniel 9:24–27. Here, Daniel hears from the angel Gabriel a vision regarding "seventy weeks" to end sin and bring reconciliation. Most agree that the seventy weeks is a literal timeline of years, not days, with the total being 490, and that most of the events have already taken place. Where theologians and biblical scholars are divided with the Seventy Weeks are when to start counting them, how to count them, when they end, and if there are any gaps in the years, like the book of Revelation possibly being an expansion of the last "week." Many of the terms in the passage are understood differently, depending on one's method of interpretation. How do you understand this passage?

October 15: The Tribulation

The Tribulation is the term for the period of judgment on the world before the kingdom. It takes up most of the book of Revelation and is referenced multiple times in Scripture (Zech. 12, 14; Mat, 24, 25; Mark 13; Luke 21). There are many views on the Tribulation and when the events take place, but there are some core concepts. The first are the seven seals (Rev. 6:1–17), which include four horsemen (Rev. 6:1–8). The seventh seal is the seven trumpets (Rev. 8–15), and the seven bowls are last (Rev. 16–18). Here, a third of the earth, sea, and sky are destroyed (Rev. 8:7–13). It is often viewed that the Tribulation occurs within seven years, and the Antichrist commits an awful act at the midway point. Where do you believe Christians are during these events?

October 16: Antichrist

The Antichrist is a central figure of evil in the Tribulation, as well as the term for those who are in opposition to Jesus Christ. The term "antichrist" only appears in the epistles of John. Here, antichrists are those that deny the Father and the Son (1Jn. 2:22), and who deny that Jesus came in the flesh (1Jn. 4:3; 2Jn. 1:7). There are many antichrists, but John reminds the church that they know an Antichrist will come in the future (1Jn. 2:22). In the book of Revelation, John also speaks about the Antichrist, but, this time, he speaks of him as *the Beast, a figure reminiscent of the four beasts in Daniel 7* (Rev. 13:1–10). The book of Daniel mentions a little horn (Dan. 7:8, 11) and a king (Dan. 11:36–45), which hold striking similarities to Antichus IV Epiphanes (215–164 BC), who sacrificed a pig in the temple. What else can we do about the Antichrist(s)?

October 17: The Kingdom

The Kingdom is the ruling and reigning of Jesus Christ as King. God was the leader of Israel until they asked Samuel for a king (1 Sam. 8:4–22). After King Saul's failed regency, God promised David that Israel will be ruled by an heir of his line (2 Sam. 7:8–17). That heir came as Jesus of Nazareth, who was heralded by His cousin John (Matt. 3:2). Jesus continued to offer up a kingdom of God (Matt. 4:17; Mark 1:15), and, either a separate or the same kingdom of heaven, which is an exclusive term to Matthew's writings and can be seen as "kingdom of God" in parallel texts (Matt. 19:14; Mark 10:14). The kingdom is often viewed as the Millennial Kingdom in Revelation 20, although some believe in *Realized Eschatology, where the kingdom is "now, but not yet."* When does Jesus reign as King?

October 18: The Millennium

The Millennium is the term for the period of time during Jesus' rule and reign as king. The passage where we get the term "Millennial Kingdom" comes from Revelation 20. Here, the term "1,000 years" is referenced five times (Rev. 20:3, 4, 5, 6, 7). In this passage, Satan is bound, and martyrs are resurrected under Jesus' reign. After the Millennium, Satan is unbound to deceive people, a battle takes place, and God judges the rest of His creatures. The issues that are debated regarding the Millennial Kingdom are: whether it takes place now, in the past, or in the future; whether the circumstances that take place in the chapter are to be understood literally or figuratively; and if the Millennium is actually one thousand years long, or a just a long period of time. Do you believe that Jesus Christ will rule and reign for a literal one thousand years?

October 19: Historic Premillennialism

Historic Premillennialism is the view that Jesus will return once before the Millennium but after the Tribulation. Historic Premillennialism is the eschatological view held by some early church fathers. Instead of a separate rapture event that takes place sometime before the Tribulation, Historic Premillennialists believe in only one event before the Millennium where Christ will return after the Tribulation and collect all believers. They also believe that, although the Church is currently acting as Israel in a spiritual sense, true, ethnic Israel will gain the Old Testament promises that God made with them in the end times. Here, the Millennial Kingdom and its events, as well as the eternal state are literal. Do you hold to Historic Premillennialism? Why?

October 20: Amillennialism

Amillennialism is the view that the Millennium and other events in the book of Revelation are figurative, that we are now in the Church Age waiting for Jesus' return, and then there is judgment leading into the Eternal State. This view was first developed by Augustine in his work *City of God*, and it was the predominant view in the Middle Ages. Amillennialism is generally idealistic in how it understands the events in the book of Revelation. Amillennialists believe that the Church will spiritually inherit the promises previously made to Israel, and that the Kingdom is taking place in some way now as well as in the future. In this view, people are growing good and evil now, but, when Christ returns, they will be judged by God before they go to Heaven or Hell. Do you hold to Amillennialism? Why or why not?

October 21: Postmillennialism

Postmillennialism is the view that Jesus will return after the Church Age, which is the current state of increasing Christendom through preaching the Gospel, and then man will be judged before the Eternal State. Because of its optimistic attitude regarding the future, Postmillennialism fell out of favor after the World Wars, but it has returned as a main view along with ideas like Theocracy and Christian Nationalism. Postmillennialists believe that passages like 1 Corinthians 10:11 and 15:24-25, not Revelation 20, are the basis for the current, increasingly positive Church Age. Postmillennialists do not hold the Tribulation to be a single event, but that the Tribulation occurs now and in past events. The Eternal State occurs after Jesus' return and God's judgment. Do you hold to Postmillennialism? Why or why not?

October 22: Dispensational Premillennialism

Dispensational Premillennialism is the view that Jesus will return first in the air for living and dead believers, then the world will go through the Tribulation, Christ will return before the Millennium, and then God will judge before the Eternal State. Dispensational Premillennialism is the most recent view (1800s), and it has made a resurgence since the 1970s. This view is regarded as the most literal reading of the book of Revelation, and it attempts to look at the events as happening in the future in chronological order. In this view, Christians will not see the Tribulation, as they are with Jesus in Heaven throughout the events of Revelation. Jesus will return and rule for a literal 1,000 years before Satan is loosed and he, his followers, and all mankind will be judged. Do you hold to Dispensational Premillennialism? Why or why not?

October 23: The Final Judgment

The Final Judgment is the time in which God will judge all mankind before the Eternal States of heaven or hell. All people will one day experience judgment before God. Jesus argues that people will know Godly people by their "fruit," or the good or bad that they do (Matt. 7:15–20). All demons and unsaved people will face judgment for sins at the Great White Throne Judgment (Rev. 20:11–15). When the Corinthian church had disputes, Paul told them they can judge others by reminding them that Christians will judge angels at the white throne judgment (1 Cor. 6:3). Christians will endure the Bema Seat of Christ for what they have done in Christ (2 Cor. 5:10; Rom. 14:10–12; 1 Cor. 3:12–15; 4:5). What judgment will you face before God?

October 24: Purgatory

Purgatory is the belief that some who die will experience a cleansing of venial sins before they can enter Heaven. The concept of purgatory is held mainly by Catholics, as well as the Orthodox church, and it is based in the view of venial, mortal, and original sin (see *Degrees of Sin*). If a Christian dies with unconfessed sins, they can see purification after death before they go to heaven. Whether purgatory is temporal or an experience outside of time is debated. There is no biblical text addressing purgatory, but it is said to be implied from the extra-biblical text of 2 Maccabees 12:42–46. Catholics have also held to the doctrine of Limbo. *Limbo is the view of a state of neutrality temporarily for saints and eternally for infants between death and the afterlife.* How can purgatory exist if we are present with the Lord in death?

October 25: Hell

Hell is the general term for the state of unbelievers after death. Although the word "hell" is used to translate many words for the afterlife in the Scriptures, the actual word "hell" is not biblical, but it is from the Norse term Hel, used for both the goddess of and the home of the dead in Norse mythology. There are four terms that we translate into hell in the Bible: *sheol*, *gehenna*, *hades*, and *tartaroo* ("cast to Tartarus"). These are abodes for the dead in Greek and Hebrew thought, and are often associated with the term "abyss." Another term, the Lake of Fire (Rev. 20:14–15; 21:8), is seen as the final place of hell and the second death in the book of Revelation. How can we rightly view the biblical concept of hell given the Bible's use of pagan terms?

October 26: Hades

Hades is the term for the temporary holding place for the dead. Hades was originally a Greek term for the subterranean holding place of the dead in Greek mythology. The New Testament writers use Hades in the same way that the Old Testament writers use *Sheol, the Hebrew term for the subterranean holding place of the dead. Tartarus, the Greek abyss that holds the Titans,* is referred to in 2 Peter 2:4 to talk about the holding place for fallen angels. Peter and Jude (Jude 1:6) both allude to the extra-biblical book of Enoch speaking of fallen angels being cast into Tartarus until the day of judgment. Another term for afterlife used in the New Testament is gehenna. *Gehenna was a fiery trash pit in the Valley of Hinnom that was sometimes used for child sacrifice.* How can we better understand Hades by studying these terms?

October 27: The Lake of Fire

The Lake of Fire is the term for the fiery pit in the book of Revelation where those who are not of God are thrown into it and separated from God for eternity. The passages that speak of the Lake of Fire are found in the book of Revelation (Rev. 20:14–15; 21:8). In these passages, being cast into the Lake of Fire is called the second death, which is the permanent separation of man from God. Not only are rebellious humans thrown into the Lake of Fire, but Satan, the beast, the false prophet, and all of hades are all cast in, as well. All of these do not have their name written in the Book of Life. Sometimes, when NT authors refer to hades or gehenna, this concept of the eternal Lake of Fire is what is meant and is translated as hell. How can unbelievers avoid this death?

October 28: Heaven

Heaven is the general term for the state of believers after death. There are three heavens mentioned in the Bible: the sky, the universe, and the spiritual realm of God. Although the term *sheol* serves as the general place of the dead in the OT, in the parable of the Rich Man and Lazarus (Luk. 16:22–23), Jesus speaks of a chasm dividing the place of evildoers from *Abraham's Bosom, where the good reside in Sheol.* After Jesus' resurrection, the term *Paradise* (*paradeisos*) is used for *the believer's place with Jesus after death* (2 Cor. 12:3–4). This term is often used for gardens, particularly the Garden of Eden, in the OT. Finally, after the events of the book of Revelation, we see in chapters 21–22 a new heaven and a new Earth replacing the old, destroyed creation. The people of God will all dwell with Him there forever. How do you view Heaven?

October 29: Temple

The Temple is the house of God and the center for worship and sacrifice to Him. The first temple of God in Scripture was the *tabernacle, the mobile tent used as the temple of the ancient Israelites* (Exod. 25–27), although some scholars see a connection between the temple and the Garden of Eden. After David's reign, there were many stationary temples: Solomon's (1 Kgs. 5–6), Ezekiel's vision of a future temple 100 times the size of Solomon's (Ezek. 40–48), Zerubbabel's rebuilding of the temple after Israel's captivity (Ezra 3:8–13; Neh. 2:12–20), and the second temple that was finished by Herod before Jesus' birth and destroyed again in 70 AD. The church is currently the temple of God (1 Cor. 3:16; 6:19). Will the new temple in the new heavens and Earth (Rev. 21) be Ezekiel's temple?

October 30: New Jerusalem

The New Jerusalem is the city of believers in the new heavens and the new Earth. Jerusalem, the capital of ancient Israel, was the city where the Temple of God was built as a solid structure during the reign of Solomon. Because of the relationship that city had with God, God's house of worship, and the people of God, the Israelites began to refer to the city as *Zion, or the ideal, shining city of peace in the future.* Jesus spoke in the Gospels about leaving to build a mansion for His followers after His ascension (John 14:1–4). In Revelation, the idealized city will be finally realized as a gigantic white cube with a foundation of colorful gemstones that will descend upon the new Earth from heaven (Rev. 21:2, 10:1–22:5). People from all nations will reside within the city and there will be a tree and river that runs through the city. How do you view this city?

October 31: New Heavens and New Earth

The New Heavens and the New Earth is the term for the final estate for all believers for all eternity. In the book of Revelation, a third of the earth, sea, and sky are destroyed during the events of the Tribulation (Rev. 8:7–13). God creates a new heaven and a new Earth at the end of the Millennial Kingdom where God and His followers can live together forever (Rev. 21:3). In this state of peace, people will no longer experience sorrow in their glorified state (Rev. 21:4). Only those who have their name written in the Book of Life will dwell with God (Rev. 21:27). Here, God will replace the light of the sun (Rev. 22:5). Although there is some description of the heavenly city, it is not certain what the new Earth will look like. How can you be in the heavenly city one day?

November: The Church

November 1: Ecclesiology

Ecclesiology is the study of the church, its governance, and practices. Since the Holy Spirit descended upon believers at Pentecost to permanently indwell all those who would believe (Acts 2), Christians have desired to better understand the Church. As the Apostles would bring the Gospel to the Jew and then the Gentile, they soon began to realize that structure was needed for groups of believers, as offices were created, ordinances were instituted, liturgies were established, and later, governmental structures were refined and debated. The debate over whether Israel and the Church are separate entities has brought debate and division to this day. How can we better understand the Church, its governance, and practices?

November 2: Covenants

Covenants are contracts made between God and His people. There are various ANE covenants, but, in Scripture, we mainly see between God and man the *Promissory*, or *Suzerain-Vassal, Covenant, where a royal figure would make agreements with land-owning citizens.* These covenants are: the *Edenic, God's promise of death upon disobedience* (Gen. 2:16–17); *Adamic, God's curse on humanity* (Gen. 3:14–19); *Noahic, God's promise for no universal floods* (Gen. 8:21—9:27); *Abrahamic, the promise of land, seed, and blessing to Israel* (Gen. 15); *Mosaic, the promise of Israel as treasure* (Exod. 20–31); *Palestinian, the promise of restoring Israel* (Deut. 30:1–9); *Davidic, the promise of a king* (2 Sam. 7:5–19); and *New Covenant, the promise for future blessing* (Jer. 31:31–34). Are there any conditions to these covenants or not?

November 3: Dispensations

Dispensations are periods of human history where God works with mankind from the basis of the revelation that they have from Him. Mankind is always justified by grace through faith in Jesus Christ (Eph. 2:8–9), but how did people have a relationship with God before the Holy Spirit's indwelling, or before the Law was given, or after their innocence in the Garden? Everyone agrees that God works in different ways at different times. And many theologians have identified various numbers of dispensations, but the common number is seven: Innocence (creation to Fall), Conscience (Fall to flood), Government (flood to Abraham), Promise (Abraham to Sinai), Law (Sinai to Pentecost), Grace (Pentecost to Millennial Kingdom), and Kingdom (Millennial Kingdom to Final State). Do you recognize the existence of dispensations?

November 4: Covenant Theology

Covenant Theology is the system of biblical interpretation that sees the Bible as separated into periods of covenants between God and Himself and God and man. There are biblical covenants between man and God in the Scriptures, but in Covenant Theology, there are three theological covenants that are recognized. The first covenant is the *Covenant of Redemption, or the agreement between God the Father and God the Son that the Son will save mankind.* Next, in human history, the *Covenant of Works is the agreement between God and Adam that man will be obedient or face separation from God.* Finally, the *Covenant of Grace, which is an agreement between God and man of Jesus' salvation of mankind.* Do you see these covenants in the narrative of Scripture?

November 5: Dispensationalism

Dispensationalism is the system of biblical interpretation that sees the Bible as separated into periods of human history where God deals with mankind from the basis of the revelation that they have from Him. Whereas Covenant Theologians see the Church as the continuation, or negatively, a replacement, of Israel, Dispensationalists see a distinction between Israel and the Church. Dispensationalists recognize both the biblical covenants and the seven dispensations, but they see the covenants after the Noahic Covenant as being specifically toward Israel. Progressive Dispensationalism and Progressive Covenantalism have sought to find a middle ground between the two major views, but most of the church still holds Dispensationalism or Covenant Theology. What view do you hold and why do you hold it?

November 6: Israel

Israel is the term for the people of God, their land, a portion of that land, and the patriarch that Israel is named after. The term "Israel" means "one who wrestles with God," and it is taken from the instance when Jacob wrestles with God and God changes Jacob's name to Israel (Gen. 32:22–32). Since then, the twelve tribes of Jacob were named Israel, there land was named Israel, and, when the nation split into two nations, the name of the northern part was named Israel. A major theological question that divides the Church is what relationship do Israel and the Church have, if they are the same thing, and who gets the promises given to Israel in the OT. One theologian, Arnold Fructenbaum, even made the new theological category of *Israelology, or the study of Israel* due to its importance in theology. What is Israel's place in the End Times?

November 7: The Church

The Church is the term for the people who are justified by faith in Christ and who have the Holy Spirit indwelling them. The church (*ecclesia*) is the body (Rom. 12:5; 1 Cor. 12:12–27; Eph. 4:16; Col. 1:18), the bride (2 Cor. 11:2; Eph. 5:25–27; Rev. 19:7–9), and the brethren (Rom. 8:29; Heb. 2:11) of Christ. The scope of the Church is that there is no distinction between Jew nor Gentile, slave nor free, male nor female (Gal. 3:28). The church is made up of members of different times and locations on the Earth, but there are also groups of believers that get together in specific times and places. These local churches worship the same God and believe many of the same doctrines, yet their worship is contextualized to their settings. How do you view the Church?

November 8: Universal Church

The Universal Church is the term for the total amount of people throughout time who have been justified by faith in Jesus Christ. The universal Church is often called the invisible Church due to the fact that no individual can see or know every Christian that exists. The Church has existed since the day of Pentecost (Acts 2), and it will continue until Jesus' return. The universal Church is a unique organization because it is not limited by geography, time, gender, ethnicity, or social status (Gal. 3:28). Instead, the universal Church is connected together by God, Himself, via the Holy Spirit. The end result of the universal Church is eternal life with God forever in Heaven, as the members of the Church will dwell in the new Jerusalem (Rev. 21–22). How can we be encouraged by the multitude of believers who share in the Holy Spirit?

November 9: Local Church

The Local Church is the group of people who have been justified by faith in Jesus Christ, and who assemble together in a physical location. This assembly is also called the visible church. Throughout the New Testament, we see the apostles carry the gospel message throughout the Roman world, creating groups of believers in every city. The groups of believers were located in cities (Jerusalem, Rome, Corinth, Ephesus, Colossae, etc.), and they had elders and deacons to provide teaching and care for their congregations. These assemblies met on Sunday, partook of the Lord's Supper, and listened to preaching from the Scriptures (Acts 20:7). These meetings have continued to this day and should not be forsaken (Heb. 10:25). What local church are you a part of?

November 10: Apostle

An Apostle is one of the leaders of the early church that was commissioned by Jesus to spread the gospel and establish churches. Apostle means "sent one," and they were originally the twelve disciples of Jesus minus Judas, who betrayed Jesus and killed himself (Matt. 27:5; Acts 1:18). In Acts, the apostles voted on replacing Judas with Matthias (Acts 1:15–26), but Paul later joined their ranks, as well. The qualifications of an apostle are found in Acts 1:21–22, with an apostle needing to have been present during Jesus' ministry on earth, seen the resurrection, and been appointed by Jesus. There are other apostles mentioned in the New Testament, but it is not clear if these hold the office of apostle or have the gifting of apostle. There are some churches that believe that the office of apostle is still for today. Do you believe apostles exist today?

November 11: Bishop

A Bishop is a term for an elder leader in the early church and became the term for a church leader in an episcopal government. The term "bishop" comes from the Old English term *biscop* by way of the Greek term *episkopos*. In the New Testament, the term was used interchangeably with the other term for pastor, which is elder. After the events of Scripture, the early church began to see bishop as a separate title for leaders who are over pastors of local congregations. Later, the office of archbishop was used for leaders over bishops, with the Pope eventually being the head bishop of the Roman Catholic Church. The question is whether this decision was a development in Church history or an original, biblical category. Do you believe this office is unique or pastoral?

November 12: Pastor

Pastor is the term for an elder who is the head of a local church. In the Bible, the title "pastor" is not used, but it comes from the Latin term for "shepherd," or the Greek *poimen*. The terms that Scripture uses for this office are elder (*presbyteros*) and overseer (*episkopos*). These terms are used interchangeably when the New Testament speaks of this office. The qualifications of a pastor in the NT are that he isn't new to the faith, is above reproach, husband of one wife, vigilant, sober-minded, not a drunkard, hospitable, able to teach, is just, holy, temperate, not a brawler, not angry, not greedy, doesn't covet, parents well, and has a good reputation with unbelievers (1 Tim. 3:2–7; Titus 1:6–9; 1 Pet. 5:1–3). Those who teach God's Word are also judged more severely (Jas. 3:1), although the desire is good (1 Tim. 3:1). Do you fit these qualifications?

November 13: Deacon

Deacon is the office of the church that is dedicated to helping meet the needs of the congregation. In the book of Acts, deacons were created to take care of congregational needs after the Hellenistic believers were feeling like the Hebrew believers were receiving preferential treatment over their widows (Acts 6:1–7). The first deacons were Stephen, Philip, Prochorus, Nicanor, Timon, Parmenas, and Nicolas. The qualifications for deacon are found in 1 Timothy 3:8–13, and they are to be serious, not double-tongued, not greedy, having a pure conscience, are blameless, husband of one wife, are good parents, have a good reputation, and are bold in faith. Deacons are important to and necessary for a healthy church. Do you meet these qualifications?

November 14: Episcopalianism

Episcopalianism is a church government structure that has a bishop or archbishop at the top of an organization with lower and lower ranks of leaders over a denomination, diocese, or church. This form of church polity had some roots that began after the events of Scripture, but the bishop did not have a separate roll from an elder until the second century. These bishops claimed to be a part of *Apostolic Succession*, where *one can trace spiritual their spiritual teaching student-by-student until ultimately from one of the twelve apostles.* This polity is traditionally held by older denominations, like the Roman Catholic and Orthodox churches, but some protestant denominations, like Methodists, hold this polity, as well. In 1054, the Orthodox Church rejected the Pope as the head of the church in the Great Schism. Do you hold to this church polity?

November 15: Presbyterianism

Prebyterianism is the church government structure that has a group of leaders over smaller and smaller regional groups over local congregations. The term for this church polity comes from one of the terms for pastor, *presbyteros*. Typically, a general assembly (national meeting) is over presbyteries (group of local churches), presbyteries are over elders, and elders are over congregations. Some Lutheran denominations also share a similar form of this government called Synodal polity, although other Lutheran sects practice forms of episcopal and congregational church governments, as well. As the name suggests, the different Presbyterian sects are the primary groups that hold to this kind of church government. Do you hold to this polity?

November 16: Congregationalism

Congregationalism is the church government structure that has the congregation make decisions for the local church, often through some sort of committee of members. Congregationalism is somewhat of a reversal of an episcopalian model, in that the power is placed not from the top-down, so to speak, but from the bottom-up. In this polity, decisions that a church is faced with are decided on by the congregation. This includes everything from allocating church finances to hiring incoming pastors. In this model, church membership is not just used in the biblical sense of a Christian attending a local body, but another, dedicated tier of attender who is aligned with a church's mission, vision, and values. This way, those who vote are those who are invested in that assembly. Do you hold to this church polity?

November 17: Eastern Orthodox Churches

Eastern Orthodox Churches are a body of ancient, regional churches that hold to the tradition of eastern Fathers. There are a couple main branches of Eastern Orthodox Churches. The Greek Orthodox Church is the oldest denomination, being refined throughout the Byzantine Empire of Constantinople (now Istanbul in Turkey), and they use Byzantine Greek for their liturgical language. The Russian Orthodox Church is the largest denomination, and they use Slavonic for their liturgy. Orthodox Churches have a weaker view of sin than the western churches, they hold tradition more authoritative than Scripture, and they have a concept called *Theosis*, which is *the idea that Christians can become more divine as they grow in grace.* Can Protestants fellowship with Orthodox Churches?

November 18: Roman Catholic Church

The Roman Catholic Church is the ancient church of Rome that holds to the tradition of the western Fathers. The Roman Church is led by the Pope, who is seen as the vicar of Christ and the successor of the Apostle Peter, who they see as the first Pope. Roman Catholic liturgy revolves around the seven sacraments, specifically the eucharist. They believe that those ordained to offices in the Catholic Church have the authority and sole ability to dispense grace to the rest of the church. Priests can also grant penance and forgiveness to Catholics. The Roman Catholic and Eastern Orthodox churches split in the Great Schism of 1054. Outside of Rome and Eastern Orthodoxy, there are other churches, like the Coptic Church of Egypt, the Ethiopic Church, and the Assyrian Church that have their own traditions. Can we fellowship with Catholicism?

November 19: Lutheranism

Lutheranism is the Protestant sect started by Martin Luther as a way to reform the Catholic Church. Martin Luther, a German Augustinian monk, learned the Greek of the NT and noticed that the Greek word *metanoia* was translated into penance in the Latin Vulgate (see *Repentance*). He posted Ninety-Five Theses to state his disagreement with this translation and with the concept of indulgences. As much as Luther tried to ground the Catholic Church in the Scriptures, the project ultimately ended in a new denomination forming. Lutherans hold to paedobaptism, a unique form of the Lord's Supper, and adhere to the Larger and Smaller Catechisms. Lutheranism is the state church of the Scandinavian countries. Can other Protestants have fellowship with the Lutherans?

November 20: Protestantism

Protestantism is the broad term for non-Catholic, Scripture-based denominations of the Church. The term "Protestant" was originally a term used by Catholics for those trying to reform the Church. These protestants, led by people like Martin Luther, John Calvin, and Ulrich Zwingli, were also called Reformers, and the time of their ministry was called the Reformation (sixteenth century). These reformers held to the five solas: *sola Christus* (Christ alone), *sola Deo gloria* (glory to God alone), *sola fide* (faith alone), *sola gratia* (grace alone), and sola scriptura (Scripture alone). The Catholic Church responded with a Counter Reformation to combat these ideas. All protestants can trace some of their lineage to the reformation, but the term "Reformed" is usually associated with the views of John Calvin. Do you hold the labels of Protestant or Reformed?

November 21: Ecumenicalism

Ecumenicalism is the view that tries to include as many denominations as possible in belief or partnership. There are positive and negative aspects to ecumenicalism. Positively, the church is called to be united, not subscribing to being a part of different tribes or factions (1 Cor. 3:3–9). After all, the church is united by the Holy Spirit, not our biology or nationality. The question is whether or not someone with theological differences is in fellowship or out of fellowship with the Church. This concept of "theological triage" typically sets beliefs into four categories: Primary beliefs that are necessary, secondary beliefs that we debate, tertiary beliefs that are convictions, and beliefs that we hold loosely. What beliefs would you put into these categories?

November 22: Liturgy

Liturgy is the order in which Christians practice their worship as a community. Christian worship ought to be orderly (1 Cor. 14:40), and in Acts 2:42–47, we see the earliest aspects of Christian worship. Here, baptized believers gathered together, listened to the Apostles' teaching, celebrated the Lord's Supper, and gave of their possessions. We know later that the day the believers gathered together was on Sunday (Acts 20:7). Singing (Eph. 5:9) and prayer (Gal. 6:2; Jas. 5:16) were also part of early worship. Later, in around AD 111, after interrogating some Christians, Pliny the Younger wrote to Emperor Trajan about Christian worship, and he recorded that they met on a particular day before dawn, sang hymns, bound themselves to an oath, and ate a meal. How does your church worship together?

November 23: Ordinances

The Ordinances are the major practices that all Christians are commanded to celebrate. In the Roman Catholic Church there are seven sacraments: Baptism, Confirmation, Eucharist (the Lord's Supper), Penance, Anointing the Sick, Holy Orders, and Matrimony. These are the avenues that the Catholic Church believes grace can be dispensed from. In Protestant Churches, the only ordinances that are practiced are baptism and the Lord's Supper, as these are the only ones repeated in Scripture. Baptism is initially commanded in the Great Commission (Matt. 28:19), and believers are continually baptized throughout the events of Acts. Partaking the Lord's Supper is also commanded of the Church (1 Cor. 11:23–26). Some churches also practice foot washing (John 13:1–17). What ordinances do you practice?

November 24: Paedobaptism

Paedobaptism is the practice where infants and children are baptized. Baptism is commanded in Scripture (Matt. 28:19), but there is a question as to whether baptism contributes to one's salvation or not. Paedobaptists believe that infants and children should be baptized for a few reasons. One is that Cornelius' whole household was baptized after he accepted the Gospel, presumably including children (Acts 10:47–48). The next is that, after circumcision was seen as no longer necessary for Gentiles (Acts 15:1–35), paedobaptists see Paul arguing that Baptism is the new circumcision (Col. 2:11–12), which was the sign of the covenant between Israel and God given to young Israelites. Some who practice this view believe that baptism enables one to believe later in life, which is why it should happen at an early age. Do you hold to this view of Baptism?

November 25: Believer's Baptism

Believer's Baptism is the practice where those who believe the Gospel message are baptized as a public sign of the Holy Spirit's indwelling them. In this view, baptism does not contribute in any way to our salvation any more than the Lord's Supper does. This way, age does not play any part in when someone should be baptized, and both young and old may partake in the ceremony. Instead, one would believe after hearing and accepting the Gospel message. Baptizing after belief tends to be a theme at least since John baptized after crying "repent for the kingdom is at hand" (Matt. 3:2). Those who hold to believer's baptism would say as the Lord's Supper symbolizes Jesus' death, Baptism symbolizes our resurrection in the Holy Spirit. Do you hold to this view?

November 26: Modes of Baptism

The Modes of Baptism that the Church practices are the methods by which one is baptized and are immersion, sprinkling, and pouring. The word *baptizo* in Greek means "to dunk," and was a term used for dyeing fabrics in the ancient world. Those who practice baptism by immersion (submersion) cite this as a reason to hold that view. Those that practice sprinkling (aspersion) cite the sprinkling of the blood of sacrifices in the temple as justification for this mode. Finally, those who argue for pouring (affusion) as a mode for baptism look at the Holy Spirit's being poured out as a reason for holding this view. If immersion were the original mode of baptism in the New Testament, sprinkling and pouring may have come from the lack of water in the arid cultures the Gospel went to. What mode of baptism do you hold to?

November 27: Transubstantiation

Transubstantiation is the belief of the Lord's Supper where the substance of the bread and wine are changed into the body and blood of Jesus Christ. Transubstantiation is the view of the Lord's Supper that is held by the Roman Catholic Church. Here, the priest, who is able to dispense grace to the church, is able to change the substance of the bread and the wine into the body and blood of Jesus while the accidents, or physical appearance, of the bread and the wine remain the same. So that elements that became Jesus' body and blood did not go to waste, a policy was made that they should be consumed by the priest, stored in a tabernacle, or destroyed. Issues with this view related to Jesus' glorified body and His finished work on the cross. Do you hold this view?

November 28: Consubstantiation

Consubstantiation (Impanation) is the belief of the Lord's Supper where the real presence of the body and blood are with the bread and the wine. This view was championed by Martin Luther and is the position of the Lutheran denominations. As Martin Luther did not believe that Roman Catholic priests held any extra power from God to dispense grace, he did not believe that anyone could change the substance of the elements. But, as he wanted to reform the church, he did hold that when Jesus told the disciples to eat His body and drink His blood (Matt. 26:26–29; Mark 14:22–24; Luke 22:19–20; 1 Cor. 11:23–26), He meant just that. The Eastern Orthodox Church also hold to a "real presence" view of communion. An issue with this view is that Jesus used similar, metaphorical language in John 6:30–65. Do you hold to this view of the Lord's Supper?

November 29: Spiritual Presence Communion

The Spiritual Presence Communion view is the belief of the Lord's Supper where Jesus' literal body and blood are not in the bread and wine, but that there is a spiritual presence of Jesus at the meal. This is the view that was held by John Calvin and has become the dominant view of "reformed" churches. In this view, Calvin fully separated any remnant of physical connection of Jesus' body and blood that was held by Catholic traditions, holding that Jesus was physically seated at the right hand of God the Father (Eph. 1:20; 1 Pet. 3:22). Instead, Calvin believed that there was a ministry of the Holy Spirit in the Lord's Supper that connected the believer to the death and resurrection of Jesus. An issue with this view is how can we have more of the Spirit be with us? Do you hold this view?

November 30: Memorial Communion

The Memorial Communion View is the belief of the Lord's Supper where the celebration is a time to remember Christ's work on the cross. This view was a view held by the reformer Ulrich Zwingli, and it is a major view in evangelical and non-denominational churches. Here, there is no extra real or spiritual presence at the supper or in the elements. Instead, the main thrust of this view is the phrase "do this in remembrance of me." In this view, as with the others, a caution is made to examine oneself to make sure that one is not unworthy and in sin, or else there is a threat of sickness or death (1 Cor. 11:26–34). This view takes Jesus' words about others consuming Himself completely metaphorically, and Christians are, instead, intended to hold the Lord's Supper as a time of contemplation. Do you hold this view of the Lord's Supper?

December: The Christian Life

December 1: The Christian Life

The Christian Life is the new life that a person has in Jesus Christ once they have accepted the Gospel. The moment that someone becomes a Christian, many things become true of them that they might not be aware of. The only way to know what these truths are is to learn about them from God's Word. After this, the believer can appropriate these truths, or take what is rightfully theirs. Then, the goal for the Christian is to continually abide in Christ day by day. This life is the new normal for a believer, not something unattainable, and, therefore, the Christian ought to rest in Christ's work of conforming them to Himself. The question that most ask is, how much do we contribute to our own sanctification, if we contribute anything at all?

December 2: Faith

Faith is the trust a Christian has in Jesus and His finished work. Many non-believers incorrectly presume that the faith is a baseless crutch that believers hold with no evidence. But this couldn't be further from the truth. The book of Hebrews defines faith as the "substance of things hoped for, the evidence of things not seen" (Heb. 11:1). But unseen things here are not false things, but non-physical truths. We have faith in many things, like a chair holding us up and not breaking when we sit down, or that the food we eat won't kill us. And we are told by God's Word, which has endured millennia of scrutiny and has brought order to the known world, about a God that answers our desire for perfection and consistency, and a historical Savior who heals our sins. How can one live without faith?

December 3: Hope

Hope is the sure confidence that believers have in the promise of glory. In modern, American culture, to hope for something is like to wish for something to be true. It is more like desiring for good fortune. But in the New Testament, we are told of Christian hope, and it is grounded in the promise of God, who cannot lie, and that it is sure (Titus 1:2; Heb. 6:18–19). The Christian hope is centered on our being with God forever in glory one day. This hope is secure because those who are justified are glorified (Rom. 8:30), we already have a new birth in Jesus' resurrection (1 Pet. 1:3), and Christ living within us through the Holy Spirit ensures this promise (Col. 1:27). We are able to rejoice in this hope no matter our circumstances (Rom. 12:12). As we experience hardship in this life, how can our sure hope help bring us peace?

December 4: Love

Love is the great care, affection, and action demonstrated in close relationships that ultimately comes from God. Some forms of love in the NT, include Godly (*agape*), romantic (*eros*), brotherly (*phileo*), and parental (*storge*). In the NT, Jesus was asked what the greatest commandment was and the answer was, "love the Lord your God with all your heart, soul, mind, and strength, and love your neighbor as yourself" (Mark 12:30–31). That golden rule was raised to new heights when Jesus told His disciples in the upper room to "love as I have loved you" (John 13:34), which is impossible apart from Him loving through us. Paul tells us that faith and hope will not be necessary one day, but love will be forever (1 Cor. 13:13). How can we love in Christ?

December 5: Peace

Peace is the state of calm and order that ultimately comes from God. In the Old Testament, the Israelites believed in a concept of *shalom* (peace), where everything would be how it ought to be. Israel never experienced lasting shalom in the Old Testament, but, in the New Testament, after the Holy Spirit was sent to believers, Paul told the Philippian church that they can have peace that surpasses all understanding (Phil. 4:7). This is because, unlike Israel, the Church has God, the source of peace, indwelling within them through the Holy Spirit. The Christian can experience actual, genuine peace in this life, but lasting peace will only be experienced in the future glorified state in heaven. In the meantime, we can live our lives in Christ and experience peace through hardships. What does living a life of peace in Christ look like?

December 6: Sabbath

Sabbath is intentional rest from work done by God, for God, and in Christ. God rested on the seventh day after He created everything (Gen. 2:2–3). This was not because God was tired, but because this demonstrated His supremacy and satisfaction over His perfect creation. God's sabbath rest set the tone for the commandment of God not to work on the seventh day (Exod. 20:8). This rest was for the Israelites to rest from their work like God, to have intentional times to be absolutely dependent on Him, and to reflect on God's supremacy in Creation. In the New Testament, the author of Hebrews speaks of Christians being able to experience rest like the Israelites could've had in entering the promised land (Heb. 4:1–13), where God does all the work necessary for us to be with Him. How can you have rest in Christ's finished work?

December 7: Joy

Joy is the state that a believer can experience when they are abiding in Christ. In the vine and the branches discourse (John 15:1–11), John records Jesus speaking of a relationship where Christians can produce fruit that is valuable to the Father when we abide in Christ. Jesus says that He tells them this so that their "joy might be full" (John 15:11). In the book of 1 John, John tells his audience of believers that he desires that they have fellowship with one another so that "their joy may be complete" (1 John 1:4). The joy in fellowship and love appears to be grounded in our abiding in Christ, and we begin that process with confession (1 John 1:9). Joy is not an emotion, but a response to our abiding fellowship. How is your abiding relationship with Christ?

December 8: Emotions

Emotions are behavioral responses to life experiences and memories. Emotions are human. As persons, we have independent minds, wills, and emotions that are subject to the different interactions that we have in this world. This means that it is normal for us to have both positive and negative emotions. Moses got angry (Num. 20:1–13), Jeremiah lamented, and Jesus wept (John 11:35). But because we are limited in understanding and the heart is deceitful, wicked, and unknowable to us (Jer. 17:9), our emotions can never be perfect in response to our experiences. Therefore, although we can have an emotional response from reading the Word or from conviction in worship or prayer, we should approach worship, like Scripture reading, with sober minds. What passages of the Bible have made you emotional when reading them?

December 9: Identity

Identity is the concept of who you are. As human beings, there is a way in which we perceive ourselves and a way in which others perceive us. Oftentimes, we try to curate our identity, especially if we do not like how we were in our past. The Bible speaks about two identities we have: our old man in Adam and our new man in Christ. Paul tells us that death reigned in all men since Adam (Rom. 5), and this is our old man, who has been crucified in Christ (Rom. 6:6) and who is corrupt and can be put off (Eph. 4:22–24). We now have died in Christ, and have a new identity in Christ, who has raised us from the dead (Rom. 6). Therefore, we do not need to create a new identity, but realize the new identity we have in Christ. How can we live this new life?

December 10: Victory

Victory is the Christian's real condition over sin and death through Jesus' finished work on the cross. Paul tells us that the Holy Spirit applies to us Jesus' victory over sin and death (1 Cor. 15:55–57; Rom. 8:2, 37; Col. 2:15), as does John (1 John 5:4). This victory is not something that the Christian has earned. Only God is able to destroy sin and death. Because Jesus is completely God and completely man, He was able to defeat sin and death on the cross. Through the mutual indwelling of the Trinity, when the Holy Spirit indwells us upon our belief in Jesus and His finished work, we gain Jesus' victory for ourselves. This victorious life is a truth that we can live out now, not just in glory. The question is whether or not we live this way. How can you live in such a way that Jesus' victory over sin and death is experienced in your life?

December 11: Exchanged Life

The Exchanged Life is the term for God's view of the Christian in Christ and Christ in the Christian. As Christ lives in us (Gal. 2:20) by faith (Eph. 3:17–19) and is the hope of glory (Col. 1:27), we also are light (Eph. 5:8), children of God (Gal. 3:26), and new creations (2 Cor. 5:17), created unto good works (Eph. 2:10), rooted and built up (Col. 2:7), blessed (Eph. 1:3), our needs are met (Phil. 4:19), have been given wisdom, righteousness, sanctification, and redemption (1 Cor. 1:30), chosen to be blameless (Eph. 1:4), have been brought near to (Eph. 2:13) and have access to God (Eph. 2:13), obtained an inheritance (Eph. 1:11), are raised and sit in heavenly places (Eph. 2:6), and receive no condemnation in Christ (Rom. 8:1). How have you been able to endure all in Christ (Phil. 4:13)?

December 12: Appropriation

Appropriation is taking what is rightfully yours. In a legal understanding, people are able to appropriate property that is already theirs under law, but they can only do so if they are aware of the property's existence. In a biblical and theological understanding, there are many blessings that are ours that we may not be aware of (Eph. 1:3, 11). We can know that we have died to sin (Rom. 6:2, 11), have been buried (Rom. 6:4), are raised with Christ to a new life (Rom. 6:5, 7), and we are seated in the heavenly places (Eph. 2:6). There is more that is true of us in Christ, but none of these truths can be experienced by our senses. Therefore, there is a process of appropriation where we must read about these truths in Scripture, understand them, believe that they are true of us, and then live in light of these truths. What biblical truths have you appropriated?

December 13: Yield

To Yield in the Christian life is to allow oneself to be used for Christ's purposes. The primary text for this concept is found in Romans 6:6–14. Here, we are to know, reckon, and then yield. We are to know that, in Christ, the old man is crucified in Christ, destroying sin as our master, and freeing us from the slavery of sin (Rom. 6:6–7). We must also know that we are not only dead, but alive through Christ's resurrection. This way, both sin and death are defeated for us (Rom. 6:8–10). Then, we must reckon that this is true of us (Rom. 6:11). Finally, we must yield not to the sin we used to, but we must live and act as instruments of God (Rom. 6:12–14). Have you known, reckoned, or yielded to this reality of sin in relationship to your new life?

December 14: Condition

The Condition of the believer is the current circumstance that a believer experiences in the Fallen world that does not align with spiritual reality. The New Testament reveals many truths of the Christian that are not experiential. There are many reasons for this. One is that our senses are relegated to material reality. Since the salvific truths that the Christian has are spiritual in nature, they cannot be felt by our senses. Second, the world is Fallen. Therefore, the things that we do experience from the physical world are tainted from sin and are often antithetical to the things God says are true of us. Because of this, if we have learned them, we often forget or disbelieve biblical truths. The answer to this problem is to remember the position that we have seated with Christ with all the blessings we have in Christ. What conditional things do you focus on?

December 15: Position

The Position of the believer is seated in the heavenlies with Christ with every spiritual blessing that does not align with their physical experience in the Fallen world. Believers that have not experienced physical death are obviously not glorified or in Heaven. But Paul tells us that, due to the Holy Spirit's ministry, we are in Christ, who is currently seated at the right hand of the Father in the Heaven (Eph. 1:3; 2:6; Col. 3:1–3). In this reality, we also have every spiritual blessing. The issue is that, because Christians live in this Fallen world, we often forget these biblical truths, and, therefore, we live in light of our condition, not our position. The remedy is to learn the things true of us and live in light of them. How can you live out the things that are true of you according to Scripture?

December 16: Purpose

The Purpose of the Christian is to glorify God. God has given many commandments to men at different times, all with the intention to worship God and to give Him the glory that is His due. One of the first repeated commandments to mankind was to "be fruitful and multiply" (Gen. 1:28; 9:1, 7). Later, the 10 Commandments were repeated to Israel as specific laws to follow out of the 613 laws of Moses (Exod. 20:3–17; Deut. 5:7–21). These laws continued into Jesus' day, yet when He asked what the "greatest" commandment was, He was given the Shema, "Love the Lord with all your heart, soul, mind, and strength" (Deut. 6:4–9; 11:13–21; Num. 15:37–41) coupled with "love your neighbor as yourself" (Lev. 19:18; Matt. 22:37–40; Mark 12:28–34; Luke 10:25–28). The Church was then given the Great Commission (Matt. 28:18–20). How do you glorify God?

December 17: Discipleship

Discipleship is the process of following and teaching other believers to follow Jesus. Jesus had twelve disciples, but the number grew to seventy during His ministry (Luke 10:1), and that number grew to one hundred and twenty by the time Judas was replaced (Acts 1:15–26). Jesus had three that were closer (Matt. 17:1–8; Mark 14:32–42), and John was the disciple that He loved (John 19:25–27). When Jesus gave the Great Commission (Matt. 28:18–20), He commanded the disciples to teach them all the things He commanded them. This seems to include the Great Commandment (Mark 12:28–34), but also the greater commandment to love as Jesus loves (John 13:34; 15:12). As we continue the Great Commission, how do you disciple other believers?

December 18: Meditation

Meditation is the active consideration and contemplation of truths found in the Scriptures. Unlike Eastern meditation, which is more of an attempt to empty your mind, biblical meditation is more like filling your mind through contemplation about a particular, biblical concept. One can meditate (*hagah*) on God (Ps. 63:6), on God's work (Pss. 77:12; 143:5), on the Scriptures (Josh. 1:8; Pss. 1:2; 119:15, 23, 48, 78, 148), as there is an entire Psalm dedicated to meditation (*siyach*) on God's Word (Ps. 119:15, 23, 48, 78), or even on an emotion response (like terror, Isa. 33:18). One does not need to meditate (*suach*) in a particular holy place (Gen. 24:63), and Christians are still to meditate on scriptural truths to this day (1 Tim. 4:15). Where do you like to contemplate scriptural truth, and what truth do you meditate on?

December 19: Prayer

Prayer is the believer speaking with God. As God's Word is God speaking to us, our response to God is our prayer to Him. The book of Psalms is a book in the Bible that is almost exclusively made up of prayers to God, and there are many famous prayers in Scripture, from Abraham (Gen. 18:16–19), Jonah (Jonah 2), Nehemiah (Neh. 9), and from Jesus, Himself (John 17), who provided the structure for prayer (Matt. 6:9–13; Luke 11:2–4). Prayers can be for requests (supplication), others (intercessory), or giving thanks to God (1 Tim. 2:1), as well as prayers of blessing, judgment (imprecatory), or praise. Jesus said prayers should be private, earnest, and succinct (Matt. 6:6–7; Luke 18:13). What does your prayer life look like? How do you pray?

December 20: Confession

Confession is the process of our telling our sins to God, and it is the first step to our abiding relationship with God in Christ. We are already "washed" but we need "cleansing" from our sins (John 13:2–11). John tells us that when we confess our sins, Jesus is faithful to cleanse us from unrighteousness (1 John 1:9). Us coming to Jesus instead of turning away from Him is crucial to our bearing fruit for God as we are in fellowship in Christ (John 15; 1 John). It is also possible for us to confess our sins to one another (Jas. 5:16), but this should be done when it is due to our sinning against each other, in the safety of righteous brethren, and not as a substitute for our confession to God. It is no benefit to the believer to keep their sins from being confessed to God, as God is already aware of our sins. Do you confess your sins to God?

December 21: Abiding

Abiding is the relationship and fellowship that we have in Christ where we are able to produce fruit for God. In John 15, Jesus likens our abiding relationship with Him as to a fruitful vine with its branches intact. The context of this passage is Jesus communicating His new commandment to love others as He loved to the disciples in the upper room before His death. The disciples would soon be receiving the Holy Spirit at Pentecost (Acts 2), and Jesus tells them that they need to abide in Him to produce fruit for God. Just like in vine dressing, branches are pruned and raised off of the ground to produce fruit, and unconnected branches are as useful as trash. How can we abide in Christ to produce fruit that is useful for God the Father?

December 22: Monasticism

Monasticism is the lifestyle where one decides to live by a religious code by themselves or within a group. Monasticism, or aestheticism, is typically practiced separate from society. The separatist, Jewish sect of the Essenes, which may also have been the Dead Sea community, may have inspired monasticism. The first Christian monk was Anthony the Great (251–356). Anthony was an Egyptian Christian who started *Eremitic Monasticism*, or *monasticism practiced in isolation*. In contrast, *Cenobitic Monasticism*, which is *monasticism practiced in groups*, is practiced with a rule, or order, and includes Benedictines, Cistercians, Franciscans, and Dominicans, to name a few. These rules revolve around worship and work. Can Christianity be practice separated from civilization?

December 23: Piety

Piety is the concept where one lives an intentionally holy and Godly life. Piety is both a concept and a movement and comes from the Latin *pius*, or devout. Pietistism came out of Lutheranism in the seventeenth century, and it was a reaction towards what was perceived as an increasingly formalistic and spiritually dead Lutheran church. Philip Spener (1635–1705) wrote a book called *Pia Desideria*, and proposed solutions to heal the church that involved more focus on Scripture and action in love for pastors and the average Christian. Piety as a concept can have a negative and a positive connotation, as people may consider the pious as more self-righteous, but, also, to take their faith more seriously. Christians can live piously by being intentional in how they live. How can we both take our faith more seriously and not to fall into self-righteousness?

December 24: Orthopraxy

Orthopraxy is the term for the correct practice of a Christian according to the Scriptures. Due to the progress of Scripture, there are commandments that Israelites are to practice under the Law in the Old Testament, and there are different practices that the Christians in the New Testament are to do. The main difference is that Christ's death and resurrection satisfy what the sacrifices in the Law could never actually satisfy, and, therefore, although the various practices of the Law showed a need for unattainable righteousness, Christ's sacrifice provided that righteousness for us. After the Bible was written, a tradition of practices was slowly built up until the Protestant Reformation brought merely scriptural practices back to the forefront. What are some scriptural practices that Christians ought to do?

December 25: Worship

Worship is the act of man showing God His due worth by performing various actions. In the Old Testament, the Israelite's duty was based around the ritual sacrifices carried out in the Law of Moses. After Christ's finished work on the cross and the Holy Spirit indwelling believers, the Church was told in the New Testament to worship God in other ways. Each Christian can worship God by being baptized individually and take the Lord's Supper corporately. When we gather together on the Lord's Day, we can also praise Him (1 Pet. 2:9), sing psalms, hymns, and spiritual songs (Eph. 5:19; Col. 3:16), pray, read and preach the Word, and provide for the care of the less fortunate (Jas. 1:27). How do you worship God in private and at your local church?

December 26: Service

Service is the concept of providing for others. People serve others in various ways. By obligation, societies have forced people to serve through slavery, and businesses have incentivized people to serve by paying them. In families, people otherwise have served their parents and siblings growing up, and they continue to serve their spouse and children when they form a new family after marriage. One may volunteer for their community, if they have an area of service that they are interested in. But what about service for love's sake? In Christ, the Christian is exhorted to serve their brother or sister in Christ, as well as the communities we live in (Rom. 12:10; Gal. 5:13; 6:2; Eph. 6:7; Phil. 2:3–4; 1 Pet. 4:10) which we do because Jesus loves through service (Matt. 25:35–40; John 13:14–15) and He lives in us. How can you serve others?

December 27: Good Works

Good Works are actions performed for God in Christ. Paul tells us that we are justified by grace through faith in Christ, not by works (Rom. 3:24; 11:6; Eph. 2:8–9; Gal. 2:16; Titus 3:5). Some have pitted James against Paul's teaching, by pointing out that James declared we are saved by works, and that faith without works is dead (Jas. 2:24, 26). They both use Abraham as an example, but Paul references God's earlier action declaring Abraham righteous through his faith (Gen. 15:6; Rom. 4:3), and James references Abraham's later action of faith (Gen. 22; Jas. 2:21). Therefore, we are not justified through works, but our works show our justification. And now, we are able to do good works in Christ (Eph. 2:10). What has God done through you to bless mankind and honor Himself?

December 28: Legalism

Legalism is the concept of holding a rigid standard of morality for yourself and/or others. Because there are various laws and commandments throughout the Scriptures, many have taken it upon themselves to attempt to master these laws and, often, expect others, saved or not, to uphold these laws to the same degree. The Pharisees are often mentioned as examples of legalism, as they did things highlighting their good works in society, upholding the letter of the Law, without seeing the spirit behind the Law, which is God and His love (Matt. 6:2; 23:23, 27). We can have this same attitude when it comes to the good works that we do for God. It is inappropriate to expect those who do not know God to live for Him, to expect others to be at our level of growth in Christ, or to presume we follow Him as well as we should. How do you struggle with this?

December 29: License

License is the concept of holding a loose standard of morality for yourself and/or others. Because Jesus Christ saved us by Grace through faith and not by works, many have presumed that there is no expectation on the Christian's part to act according to what Christ has commanded us. It is true that Christ fulfilled the Law (Matt. 5:17), and Christians are now under grace (Rom. 6:14). But this does not mean there is nothing for the Christian to do now in Christ. Paul argued that we should not live carnally to highlight God's grace, but instead, we are now able to do good works in Christ when we could not do so before salvation (Rom. 6). There are also the many commands in the NT to live in Christ and do good. How have you struggled with licentiousness?

December 30: Liberty

Liberty is the concept of holding an appropriate standard of morality for yourself and/or others. Because the options of legalism and licentiousness are not consistent with how a Christian ought to walk, there should be a third way of living that is representative of how Christians should carry out their walk in Christ. Paul tells the Corinthian church that they have liberty in Christ (1 Cor. 8:9; 2 Cor. 3:17). There are expectations that we have regarding the liberty we have in Christ. Even though Christians have liberty, some actions we do may be considered immoral by non-Christian morality. And if people with these non-Christian morals see Christians perform these actions, they can believe God is immoral because of us (Gal. 2:4; 5:13; Jas. 1:25; 2:12; 1 Pet. 2:16). In our freedom, what things can we abstain from doing so others do not stumble?

December 31: Rewards

Rewards are the good or bad achievements received by all people after the Day of Judgment. We are told in 1 Cor. 3:12–15 that, depending on what one has done in this life, one will receive incorruptible and valuable rewards for their good work (1 Cor. 3:8, 14; Col. 2:18; 3:24; Heb. 10:35; 1 Pet. 1:7; 2 John 1:8; Rev. 22:12), or corruptible and worthless rewards for their bad works (Rom. 4:4; 2 Tim. 4:14; 2 Pet. 2:13). There are a few times that crowns are used as a stand-in for our rewards. These are: an incorruptible crown (1 Cor. 9:25), a crown of rejoicing (1 Thess. 2:19), a crown of righteousness (2 Tim. 4:8), a crown of life (Jas. 1:12; Rev. 2:10), and a crown of glory (1 Pet. 5:4). These rewards are seen as a motivator for the Christian to live their life in Christ. What rewards do you believe you will receive?

Appendix: Class Schedule

This schedule is designed for a church to have a class or small group go through this book for 48 weeks of the year. You can always choose just one month to go through. But this schedule goes through the whole book from January to December and takes a week off each for Christmas in Winter, Easter in Spring, VBS or 4th of July in Summer, and Launch or Thanksgiving in Fall. As there are 13 weeks every season, this schedule has one class every week for 12 weeks per season:

1. January Week 1: The Bible, 1–8
2. January Week 2: The Bible, 9–16
3. January Week 3: The Bible, 17–24
4. January Week 4: The Bible, 25–31
5. February Week 1: Humanity, 1–7
6. February Week 2: Humanity, 8–14
7. February Week 3: Humanity, 15–21
8. February Week 4: Humanity, 22–28
9. March Week 1: God the Father, 1–8
10. March Week 2: God the Father, 9–16
11. March Week 3: God the Father, 17–24
12. March Week 4: God the Father, 25–31
13. April Week 1: God the Son, 1–7
14. April Week 2: God the Son, 8–15
15. April Week 3: God the Son, 16–23
16. April Week 4: God the Son, 24–30

17. May Week 1: God the Spirit, 1–8
18. May Week 2: God the Spirit, 9–16
19. May Week 3: God the Spirit, 17–24
20. May Week 4: God the Spirit, 25–31
21. June Week 1: Angels, 1–7
22. June Week 2: Angels, 8–15
23. June Week 3: Angels, 16–23
24. June Week 4: Angels, 24–30
25. July Week 1: Civics, 1–8
26. July Week 2: Civics, 9–16
27. July Week 3: Civics, 17–24
28. July Week 4: Civics, 25–31
29. August Week 1: Sin/Salvation, 1–8
30. August Week 2: Sin/Salvation, 9–16
31. August Week 3: Sin/Salvation, 17–24
32. August Week 4: Sin/Salvation, 25–31
33. September Week 1: Creation, 1–7
34. September Week 2: Creation, 8–15
35. September Week 3: Creation, 16–23
36. September Week 4: Creation, 24–30
37. October Week 1: End Times, 1–8
38. October Week 2: End Times, 9–16
39. October Week 3: End Times, 17–24
40. October Week 4: End Times, 25–31
41. November Week 1: The Church, 1–7
42. November Week 2: The Church, 8–15
43. November Week 3: The Church, 16–23
44. November Week 4: The Church, 24–30
45. December, Week 1: Christian Life, 1–8
46. December, Week 2: Christian Life, 9–16
47. December, Week 3: Christian Life, 17–24
48. December, Week 4: Christian Life, 25–31

Bibliography/Book Recommendations

Systematic Theology

Ryrie, Charles C. *Basic Theology: A Popular Systematic Guide to Understanding Biblical Truth.* Chicago: Moody, 1999. A basic introduction. Start here.

Geisler, Norman. *Systematic Theology.* 4. vols. Bastion, 2025. I highly recommend Geisler's 4-volume set. Analytic and great for apologetics.

Grudem, Wayne. *Systematic Theology: An Introduction to Biblical Doctrine.* 2nd ed. Grand Rapids: Zondervan Academic, 2020. Grudem's text is best for providing the systematic theologies of other denominations in each chapter, as well as hymns and reflection questions.

Additions and Counterpoints

Clark, David K. *To Know and Love God: Method for Theology.* Wheaton, IL: Crossway, 2010.

Multiple Authors. *A Handbook of Theology.* Edited by Daniel L. Akin, David S. Dockery, and Nathan A. Finn. Theology for the People of God. Nashville: B&H Academic, 2023. These two books are great for theological method.

Bibliology

Dockery, David S., and Malcolm B. Yarnell III. *Special Revelation and Scripture.* Theology for the People of God. Nashville: B&H Academic, 2024.

Feinberg, John S. *Light in a Dark Place: The Doctrine of Scripture.* Foundations of Evangelical Theology. Wheaton, IL: Crossway, 2018.

Hendricks, Howard G., and William D. Hendricks. *Living by the Book: The Art and Science of Reading the Bible.* Chicago: Moody, 2007. In my opinion, this is the best introduction to hermeneutics.

Additions and Counterpoints

Kitchen, Kenneth A. *On the Reliability of the Old Testament.* Grand Rapids: Eerdmans, 2006. Archaeological apologetic.

Kruger, Michael J. *Canon Revisited: Establishing the Origins and Authority of the New Testament Books.* Wheaton, IL: Crossway, 2012. A help for understanding the canon.

Anthropology

Farris, Joshua R. *An Introduction to Theological Anthropology: Humans, Both Creaturely and Divine.* Grand Rapids: Baker Academic, 2020.

Hammett, John S., and Katie J. McCoy. *Humanity.* Theology for the People of God. Nashville: B&H Academic, 2023.

Poythress, Vern S. *Making Sense of Man: Using Biblical Perspectives to Develop a Theology of Humanity.* Phillipsburg, NJ: P&R, 2024.

Additions and Counterpoints

Craig, William Lane. *In Quest for the Historical Adam: A Biblical and Scientific Exploration.* Grand Rapids: Eerdmans, 2021.

Swamidass, S. Joshua. *The Genealogical Adam & Eve: The Surprising Science of Universal Ancestry.* Downers Grove, IL: IVP Academic, 2021. This book and Craig's have both been controversial in what they put forth, but they are both Christian and sympathetic to macro-evolution, and, therefore, they provide great counterpoints.

Theology Proper

Feinberg, John S. *No One Like Him: The Doctrine of God.* Foundations of Evangelical Theology. Wheaton, IL: Crossway, 2006. Worth its weight in gold.

Packer, J. I. *Knowing God.* 50th anniversary ed. Downers Grove, IL: IVP, 2023. A more pastoral approach to theology proper.

Yarnell, Malcolm B., III. *God.* Theology for Every Person. Nashville: B&H, 2024.

Additions and Counterpoints

Craig, William Lane. *Time and Eternity: Exploring God's Relationship to Time.* Wheaton, IL: Crossway, 2001.

Litfin, Bryan M. *The Story of the Trinity: Controversy, Crisis, and the Creation of the Nicene Creed.* Grand Rapids: Baker, 2025. History of trinitarian formulation.

Christology

Akin, Daniel L. *Christology: The Study of Christ.* The Concise Theology Series. Nashville: Rainer, 2015.

Pentecost, J. Dwight. *The Words and Works of Jesus Christ.* Grand Rapids: Zondervan Academic, 2000.

Walvoord, John F. *Jesus Christ our Lord.* Chicago: Moody, 1969.

Additions and Counterpoints

Bauckham, Richard. *Jesus and the Eyewitnesses: The Gospels as Eyewitness Testimony.* Grand Rapids: Eerdmans, 2017.

Wright, N. T. *The Resurrection of the Son of God.* Christian Origins and the Question of God 3. Philadelphia: Fortress, 2003.

Pneumatology

Allison, Gregg R. and Andreas J. Kostenberger. *The Holy Spirit.* Theology for the People of God. Nashville: B&H Academic, 2020.

Cole, Graham A. *He Who Gives Life: The Doctrine of the Holy Spirit.* Foundations of Evangelical Theology. Wheaton, IL: Crossway, 2007.

Ryrie, Charles C. *The Holy Spirit.* Chicago: Moody, 1997.

Additions and Counterpoints

Gaffin, Richard B., Jr., Robert L. Saucy, C. Samuel Storms, and Douglas A. Oss. *Are Miraculous Gifts for Today? Four Views.* Grand Rapids: Zondervan Academic, 1996.

Kärkkäinen, Veli-Matti. *The Holy Spirit: A Guide to Christian Theology.* Louisville: Westminster John Knox, 2012. A Charismatic-Pentecostal approach.

Angelology, Demonology, and Satanology

Cole, Graham A. *Against the Darkness: The Doctrine of Angels, Satan, and Demons.* Foundations of Evangelical Theology. Wheaton, IL: Crossway, 2019.

Heiser, Michael. *The Unseen Realm: Discovering the Supernatural World of the Bible.* Expanded ed. Bellingham, WA: Lexham, 2025.

Additions and Counterpoints

Heiser, Michael S. *Angels: What the Bible Really Says about God's Heavenly Host.* Bellingham, WA: Lexham, 2018.

Heiser, Michael S. *Demons: What the Bible Really Says about the Powers of Darkness.* Bellingham, WA: Lexham, 2020.

Political Theology

Grudem, Wayne. *Politics According to the Bible: A Comprehensive Resource for Understanding Modern Political Issues in Light of Scripture.* Grand Rapids: Zondervan, 2010. From a politically conservative theology scholar.

Longman, Tremper, III. *The Bible and the Ballot: Using Scripture in Political Decisions.* Grand Rapids: Eerdmans, 2020. From a politically liberal Bible scholar. Between this and the previous work, one can see a good spectrum of political conclusions.

Additions and Counterpoints

The United States' Declaration of Independence and the Constitution of the United States. These should be owned, read, and understood by all Americans. It is also wise to read the Articles of Confederation, as well.

The Federalist Papers. If possible, read these and papers by the Anti-Federalists, as well. These are all papers either written to promote or reject the passing of the Constitution. All of these American State papers are used in legal decisions.

Hamartiology and Soteriology

Chafer, Lewis Sperry. *Salvation.* Chicago: Moody, 1944.

Demarest, Bruce. *The Cross and Salvation: The Doctrine of Salvation.* Foundations of Evangelical Theology. Wheaton, IL: Crossway, 2006.

McCall, Thomas H. *Against God and Nature: The Doctrine of Sin.* Foundations of Evangelical Theology. Wheaton, IL: Crossway, 2019.

Additions and Counterpoints

Craig, William Lane. *Atonement and the Death of Christ: An Exegetical, Historical, and Philosophical Exploration.* Waco, TX: Baylor University Press, 2020.

Olson, C. Gordon. *Beyond Calvinism and Arminianism: An Inductive Mediate Theology of Salvation.* 3rd ed. expanded, revised, and updated. Minneapolis: Global Gospel Publishers, 2018. This book provides counterpoints to both the Calvinistic and Arminian frameworks. A more abbreviated work called *Getting the Gospel Right: A Balanced View of Calvinism and Arminianism* also exists.

Creation

Duncan, J. Ligon, David W. Hall, Hugh Ross, Gleason L. Archer, Lee Irons, and Meredith G. Kline. *The Genesis Debate: Three Views on the Days of Creation*. Irvine, CA: Crux, 2000.

Ham, Ken, Hugh Ross, Deborah B. Haarsma, and Stephen C. Meyer. *Four Views on Creation, Evolution, and Intelligent Design*. Grand Rapids: Zondervan Academic, 2017.

Nelson, Paul, Robert C. Newman, and Howard J. Van Till. *Three Views on Creation and Evolution*. Grand Rapids: Zondervan Academic, 1999.

Additions and Counterpoints

Behe, Michael J. *Darwin's Black Box: The Biochemical Challenge to Evolution*. NY: Touchstone, 1998.

Darwin, Charles. *On Origin of the Species: By Means of Natural Selection, or the Preservation of Favoured Races in the Struggle for Life*. Multiple formats. 1859.

Eschatology

Benware, Paul N. *Understanding End Times Prophecy*. Revised and expanded. Chicago: Moody, 2006.

Erickson, Millard J. *A Basic Guide to Eschatology: Making Sense of the Millennium*. Grand Rapids: Baker, 1998.

Pentecost, J. Dwight. *Things to Come: A Study in Biblical Eschatology*. Grand Rapids: Zondervan Academic, 1965.

Additions and Counterpoints

Blaising, Craig, Alan Hultberg, and Douglas Moo. *Three Views on the Rapture: Pretribulation, Prewrath, or Posttribulation*. Grand Rapids: Zondervan Academic, 2010.

Boettner, Loraine, Anthony A. Hoekema, Herman A. Hoyt, and George Eldon Ladd. *The Meaning of the Millennium: Four Views*. Downers Grove, IL: IVP Academic, 1977.

Ecclesiology

Allison, Gregg R. *Sojourners and Strangers: The Doctrine of the Church*. Foundations of Evangelical Theology. Wheaton, IL: Crossway, 2012.

Saucy, Robert L. *The Church in God's Program*. Chicago: Moody, 1972.

Additions and Counterpoints

Bock, Darrell, Michael Horton, Stephen Wellum, and Mark Snoeberger. *Covenantal and Dispensational Theologies: Four Views on the Continuity of Scripture*. Downers Grove, IL: IVP Academic, 2022.

Fruchtenbaum, Arnold G. *Israelology: The Missing Link in Systematic Theology*. San Antonio: Ariel Ministries, 1994. A necessary addition to a theological library.

The Christian Life

Dieter, Melvin E., Anthony Hoekema, Stanley M. Horton, J. Robertson McQuilken, and John F. Walvoord. *Five Views on Sanctification*. Grand Rapids: Zondervan Academic, 1996.

Stanford, Miles J. *The Complete Green Letters*. Grand Rapids: Zondervan, 1984.

Hull, Bill. *The Complete Book of Discipleship: On Being and Making Followers of Christ*. Colorado Springs: NavPress, 2006

Subject Index

Scripture Index

OLD TESTAMENT

Genesis

Exodus

Leviticus

Numbers

Deuteronomy

Joshua

Judges

Mark

Luke

John

Acts

Romans

Romans (*continued*)

1 Corinthians

2 Corinthians

Galatians

Ephesians

Philippians

Colossians

www.ingramcontent.com/pod-product-compliance
Lightning Source LLC
LaVergne TN
LVHW050646100826
845148LV00011B/1999

* 9 7 9 8 3 8 5 2 7 5 8 6 1 *